I0628605

SAUNDERS BOOKS IN PSYCHOLOGY

Lewis F. Petrinovich

Robert D. Singer

Consulting Editors

HARRY KAUFMANN, Ph.D.

Professor of Psychology
Hunter College of the City
University of New York

Introduction to the Study of Human Behavior

W. B. SAUNDERS COMPANY
Philadelphia   London   Toronto

W. B. Saunders Company: West Washington Square
Philadelphia, Pa. 19105

12 Dyott Street
London, WC1A 1DB

1835 Yonge Street
Toronto 7, Ontario

Introduction to the Study of Human Behavior   SBN 0-7216-5300-6

Print No.:   9   8   7   6   5   4   3

Preface

The aims of this volume

This volume is not a textbook for the many fields with which the behavioral sciences in general, and psychology in particular, are concerned. It is, instead, a statement of the premises and assumptions underlying such studies, and an examination of some of the most frequent doubts and objections to these studies, (As we shall see, criticisms and objections are by no means limited to non-scientists).

Although the profession and, possibly, the prejudices of the writer cannot remain long concealed, this book will attempt to present something other than a hymn of praise to the behavioral sciences and their followers. A substantial and, it is hoped, straightforward effort will be made to examine not only the insights we have gained in the past few decades about the behavior of organisms, but also some of the less tightly reasoned assertions which are sometimes offered under the guise of solidly demonstrated truths.

The book tries to be many things to many people. The risk is great; it is difficult to avoid both the abstruse language of narrow specialization and the dreary glibness of the popularizer; to walk the razor's edge, being neither dry nor vapid, allowing the reader glances at vast erudition gracefully borne, and flavoring urbane solemnity with dashes of elegant, but not frivolous wit. It has been often tried, rarely with success. Too often the writer is dismissed by his academic colleagues as a hack, without endearing himself to the intelligent layman as a persuasive and intelligible communicator. Sitting thus huddled in the cold between two camps, an outcast from both, he has neither the respect of his peers, nor the sun of popularity (and the usually resulting wealth) to keep him warm.

Yet, enough books have been written for the incipient and advanced behavioral scientist in language inaccessible to others, and ignorance about even his most general aims is still widespread. This state of affairs is not healthy. The value and effectiveness of a field of knowledge do not, of course, depend upon the degree of vast popular acclaim it receives, but the intelligent public's awareness is both necessary and desirable, for several reasons.

First, though the sheer vastness of knowledge has eliminated the universally educated Renaissance Man, there is no reason why specialists in any area should not endeavor to communicate, to those who care, their aims and methods. In a free society, obscurity deliberately cultivated, or even arising out of the specialist's indifference to the views of others, has no place. The scientist, as does any other citizen, owes the society in which he works an account of his activities, and is not immune to its criticism. This does not mean, of course, that the scientist must debate the ignoramus in the market place, but simply that the ethics and goals of scientific research should not be established and controlled solely from within. The scientist (perhaps to the surprise of many) is human, and the instances of a group, professional, ethnic, religious, or other, policing itself without gravely infringing upon the rights of others are deplorably few.

At the same time, the scientist, in order to work at optimal efficiency, must find himself in a psychologically favorable environment. He may not seek popular adulation, but a climate of respect and confidence will show up advantageously in both his working conditions and his own dedication. Such trust and respect must be based upon understanding, not fear, suspicion, and ignorance.

Furthermore, even the "pure" scientist develops his interests not in a vacuum, but through his contact with the world at large, and quite often with that much maligned source, "common sense." Isolation, self-imposed or enforced by others, frequently impairs the development of scientific inquiry. Though this writer is prepared to argue passionately against the proposition that scientific inquiry should always be in some way "useful" or related to immediate practical needs, it would be quite fallacious to conclude that the systematic severing of communication lines between the scientist and the rest of humanity therefore ensures scientific excellence.

These pages are meant for those who are about to enter any field of the behavioral and social sciences, and those who, having entered such a field not too long ago, find the concepts and the logic of their studies dry, forbidding, and, seemingly, quite remote from the various facets of humanity to which they purport to be related. However, the book is also addressed to the layman, not as a plea for tolerance, or a self-justifying polemic, but simply as one of the reports providing the responsible citizen in our society with the information he must have, if he is to contribute toward the crucial choices which will determine the present and future state of our society and mankind.

Harry Kaufmann

New York

Contents

CHAPTER 1

Some Problems of Knowledge

WHO WANTS TO KNOW?   WHAT CAN BE KNOWN? HOW CAN IT BE KNOWN?

Strangely enough, most people, even those who either have never heard of the Scientific Method (or, if they have, could not care less) do want to understand the world about them. Indeed, this urge to know is present also in animals; a monkey, or even a rat, will sometimes go to a great deal of trouble merely in order to explore a part of its surroundings.

In people the urge is strong, though highly diversified. Some study birds, others enjoy reading obituary notices. And aside from other interests, most people like to understand other people (as well as themselves). Quite often someone asks himself, "Now, why did he do that?" or even, "What made me say such a thing?" Sometimes this curiosity may be just "idle," but more frequently we try to understand the other person—or ourselves—in order to draw certain consequences, to make predictions about impending events, and devise subsequent action.

Knowing about, and understanding others, is necessary to live with any degree of success or satisfaction in a social environment, even though in some situations a sensitivity to the feelings of others is relatively unimportant. In a situation where everybody's behavior is precisely "programmed" or determined by simple established rules, and does not depend upon what others say or do, people can interact by relying solely upon those rules. For instance, even a person

1

largely devoid of any understanding of human behavior and motives can probably negotiate a purchase of postage stamps quite successfully. He places his money on the counter, asks for the desired denominations, and leaves. A stamp vending machine would provide the same service and require as little interpersonal skill. On the other hand, we are often faced with social situations in which the words and actions of each participant depend in a very sensitive way upon what the others say or do. Many of us, in fact, consider ourselves quite adroit in dealing with such situations. We consider ourselves good judges of "human nature."

This desire to understand people, which is thus often accompanied by a strong belief in one's powers of insight and understanding of others, can also be quite a drawback. Many reasonable people who would not dream of claiming any great expertness in botany (even though they have looked at, and even eaten, vegetables all their lives) will be quite persuaded that they possess a deep fund of psychological knowledge, simply because they have associated with people all their lives. (In fact, they might say, some of their best friends are people.) Thus, the scientific study of Man may appear to deal with the obvious, in that it tells us either what everyone already knows, or offers outlandish and erroneous ideas. I shall try to show in this book that not all worthwhile knowledge about people is obvious, and that, strangely, much "obvious" knowledge is often false or trivial. But two preliminary problems must first be settled, namely the questions of the existence of the universe, and the acquisition of knowledge.

PROBLEMS OF KNOWLEDGE

Before examining the ways in which we acquire knowledge and their sources, it is perhaps useful to determine whether it is reasonable to assume that we can obtain any kind of knowledge at all, and what the value of such knowledge might be, even if it were contended that such knowledge can be obtained.

The ontological problem, or "What exists?"   Descartes' well-known basic assumption: "I think, therefore I am," originated from a long-standing problem emphasized by the theology of the Christian Church. How can "mind" know "matter," or, in other words, how can we know anything about the world at all? Perhaps it is merely a figment of our imagination! Descartes' answer was ingenuous and persuasive; it continues to sidetrack philosophers and scientists even today. Let me assume, he said, nothing at all about the universe, except the indisputable fact that I am thinking, here and now, and that, since I am thinking, there must be an entity which does the thinking, namely I. Moreover, there must be a part of me which "knows," and a (baser) part, which is, like everything else, an object of knowledge. But immediately Descartes was faced with a further problem: What if only I exist, and the rest of the universe exists only in my thought processes? Descartes was deeply troubled by this possibility (which was later called solipsism), because to a religious philosopher who could not doubt the existence of God, questioning the existence of the universe implied that God might be playing a shabby trick of misrepresentation. It is important to realize that the step from "I think, therefore I am" to "The universe exists" does not follow logically; it follows only if the additional premises: "God exists and is infinitely good and honest," and "God provides me with perceptions of the world," are assumed. Gorgias, the sophist, summed up the dilemma 2,500 years ago: "Nothing exists. If anything existed, it could not be known. If anything could be known, it could not be communicated." He was not particularly interested in logical and theological dilemmas, and man's concern with the spiritual submerged the issue until the 17th century. Even then, the ultimate logical conclusion, that nothing exists except the mind of the perceiver, was avoided by Descartes, Leibnitz, and Berkeley. For them, God comes to the rescue: If the world appears to be there, it must be so, for to paraphrase Descartes: God is no confidence trickster. Solipsism, in denying the existence of the universe, is therefore atheistic, and conversely, traditional theism necessitates the assumption that the universe is real. (One might argue that solipsism results in a form of theism which we might call "auto-theism," meaning "I am the God of my own universe." But this variant could hardly be considered "traditional.") Today, the exact sciences have largely exorcised the ultimate doubt about the existence of the world as an insoluble metaphysical teaser. No answer can ever be proved or disproved.

The Epistemological problem: "How do we gain knowledge?" A more enduring, indeed quite fashionable, objection arises from Gorgias' second and third statements. How, if at all, can anything be known and communicated? The first of these two problems forms the basis of Kant's system. We can know, he argued, only the impressions of things, but not the things themselves. Moreover, these impressions are perceived only by virtue of their being ordered or categorized according to certain innate criteria of the perceiving mind. Any attempt to use empirical methods in order to get beyond "mere" appearances, at the "things themselves," can only result in pointless and abstruse speculation. Kant, although he wanted to provide rigorous guidelines for the acquisition of knowledge, really provided a choice for the scientist, and an alibi for the metaphysician. The scientist either had to relinquish his endeavor of knowing the world or rephrase his questions, so as to admit that he could never know more than appearances. On the other hand, the metaphysician and the theologian could comfortably ignore empirically established relationships by asserting that these relationships really tell nothing about the nature of things themselves, only of their projections. Even without questioning the existence of the world, it can be seen how Kant's distinction of perceived phenomena as opposed to "real" things had to lead to the next logical step: Perceptions and observations are intimate, personal events, which, by definition, cannot be shared directly. (Somebody else's perception becomes, therefore, a projection which can be known by me only as a "second order" projection.) Certain logical problems, for instance whether one's own mind is observer, or observed, or both, need not concern us here. Let us instead examine the argument that, since we can know nothing of what is "out there," all we can know is learned by observing and analyzing our own perceptions, or those innate ideas which may be in us.

Assuming that we know nothing about the "real" world, only what we observe inside ourselves, it is nevertheless indisputable that most of us, most of the time, act as if we expected these perceptions and observations to occur in a quite orderly manner, or rather, to use the frightening but accurate terms, as if our perceptions give at least the illusion of *causation* and *determinism*. When we fail to draw the consequences of this "illusion," a very unpleasant perception, such as that caused by a perceived, but allegedly not necessarily existing truck rolling over us, may result. Admittedly, the fact that perceptions occur in this orderly manner does not *prove* the "real" existence of the truck. We can also, in exceptional situations, choose to cultivate perceptions regardless of their orderliness, as happens in a delirium or under the influence of a psychedelic drug. But it is precisely the difference between these latter experiences and the orderly ones of our waking life which forces us to make a choice. We can never *know* whether our private perceptions are entirely the product of a deceitful, supernatural conjurer, or whether some consistent relationship exists between what is out there and what is in our brain. Our alternatives are either to act as if it were possible to know, or to resign ourselves to what is, in effect, solipsism. If we choose the latter, the next obvious step would then be to impose our choice upon our perceptions, and perceive our self-made universe according to our desires. Very few of us are able to do that, and those who do are not viewed by others with equanimity. They tend to be seen as having delusions.

Without, therefore, making too daring a leap, it might be reasonable, or at least convenient, to assume that the universe exists, that it is, at least to some extent, orderly, and that it can, at least to some extent, be known.

SOURCES OF KNOWLEDGE

As I pointed out at the beginning of the chapter, knowledge-seeking behavior is as characteristic of the primitive aborigine as of the sophisticated New Yorker (in fact, it is by no means limited to Man). The motives for seeking knowledge need not be the same; they may range from basic physical needs to a satisfying sense of mastery. Some of the ways in which knowledge has been courted by Man strike us as amusing today; the entrails of animals are no longer a generally accredited method of predicting the future (tea leaves are still quite popular, though). But magic, as a manner of acquiring knowledge, need not always be spectacular in its procedures, nor can it be said with certainty that such knowledge is always necessarily wrong. The defining characteristic, and that which distinguishes it from scientific procedures, is that a relationship between events is assumed to exist which is purely speculative, and not subjected to critical verification. Also, the manner in which one event is assumed to affect another has no basis in known natural laws; the *manner* in which, say, the stars are supposed to affect human destiny, is not specified.

We should not fall into the error of deriding the attempts of some cultures in their early stages of development to acquire mastery of their environment by the occasional use of magic. Some aspects of science itself developed out of magic, and whatever the dissimilarities, it shares with magic the urge to know the physical (as opposed to the metaphysical) world, and the belief that Man can be more than a passive, uncomprehending thing in it. A far more pernicious influence is exerted by those who claim they have come to know the nature of the universe by thinking about it intensely, or through direct inspiration by a supernatural agent. The scientist does not necessarily maintain that the only worthwhile knowledge is empirical; he may frequently be a person deeply concerned with spiritual values. But when he seeks to discover the functionings of the real, tangible world, he must, above all, be ready to observe that world, and his inferences must be consistent with such observation.

Finally, arguments are sometimes offered telling us that it is either absurd or sinful to study the nature of Man. There are only two possible rebuttals to these two viewpoints. The scientist must, first of all, show that his methods enhance our knowledge of Man, and he must demonstrate that knowledge is preferable to ignorance.

These are the major tasks of the remainder of this book.

CHAPTER 2

The Scientist and His Methods

SCIENCE AND COMMON SENSE: ENEMIES OR COUSINS?

There are, as we have seen, people who completely reject the methods and goals of science. Theirs is the life of complete renunciation toward the endeavors of Man: The life of the spirit engages their full and continuous attention. They are mystics, zealots, or, in some extreme instances, artists or poets. Others seek to make the world predictable or to make the occurrence of a desired event more likely through exhortation, magic or prayer. Many more, however, express contempt or fear of science and the scientist, and sometimes write books to that effect, while freely utilizing the scientific discoveries which have become an integral part of our Western cultural heritage. In many instances they are aware of their inconsistency, but minimize it as being irrelevant. Yet, they would not dream of entering an automobile—let alone an airplane—that has been constructed according to rules other than "scientific" ones (we shall see in a minute why the quotation marks); they drink milk which is pasteurized, they allow themselves to be vaccinated, and, even though the frequent mistakes of the meteorologist are an obvious object of ridicule, when a hurricane is forecast, most of our inconsistent sceptics make the necessary provisions, regardless of whether neighbor Jones' dog is eating grass or not. This is a short book—other examples which illustrate such inconsistency have to be left to the reader's imagination. But the point has been made: Most people, most of the time, avail themselves of "scientific" knowledge. One more counter argument comes to mind: The artisan who builds a magnificent boat, easily maneuverable and highly stable, without knowing anything about hydraulics, or the farmer whose cows are healthy and whose milk requires no pasteurization. Here the critic usually finds the ground for his defense: What does "know-how" have to do with science? If he is spirited in his arguments he will adduce the familiar examples of the physicist who cannot handle a screwdriver or build a radio, and the biologist whose pets die of mysterious ailments. It is through long-term experience or our accumulated fund of common sense, he might say, that some people build excellent tables without a knowledge of either botany or statics.

Both arguments—that which claims that know-how is a preferable substitute for science, and the one which derides scientists for their lack of practical skills—miss the point completely. The botanist or the physicist are not necessarily skillful in constructing a serviceable item of furniture. The personal lives of, say, physiologists are not greatly altered by their knowledge of the effects of various vitamins upon the functioning of the body. Much of our knowledge in many areas does not affect our own lives directly and powerfully, sometimes because we may not have sufficient opportunities to apply it. The psychologist may not be at home enough to apply his knowledge to the rearing of his children; furthermore, too many uncontrollable variables are present; the psychologist's unruly child experiences encounters with many people from whom he might learn inappropriate behaviors. Finally, we do not always act in accordance with what we know to be best. Physicians smoke even though they should know better, and psychologists sometimes are angry, or fearful, or jealous, though they might be quite able to explain the reasons for their feelings.

In spite of all this, technological know-how and a skill derived from years of trial and error are not substitutes for scientific knowledge. We correctly speak of the latter only when we wish to imply a method of understanding and explaining relationships among events. The biologist specializing in that field understands and can explain why grass from certain types of soil makes the farmer's cattle thrive, and in what manner certain germs or viruses produce diseases. Keeping in mind again that physical scientists nowadays concentrate on areas of specialization much narrower than the layman realizes, a particular physicist can state in exact mathematical terms the relationship between heat and the expansion of a gas. None of this either implies or requires that the biologist make a good farmer, or the physicist a competent automobile mechanic.

On the other hand, there exists a bond among the scientists I have taken as my examples which does not exist between the farmer and the automobile mechanic. This common characteristic is the style or method by which knowledge is sought. You may have observed this at a cocktail party: Dr. A, who is a solid state physicist, meets Dr. B, whose specialty is microbiology, and although neither has the least knowledge about the content matter of the other, they will soon ask each other questions which are to them meaningful and intelligent. The reason for this communion is that they speak the common language of the scientific method. Knowing nothing about each other's area of competence, they are still able to communicate the manner in which problems are posed and questions answered. The language they share is the language of science.

Science, as one of its tasks, seeks to understand, explain and predict the events that occur in our world. The words "understand" and "explain" are not synonymous. "Understanding" here is meant as a simple post facto account. We observe little Johnny throwing a temper tantrum, and we may seek to *understand* what events led to this behavior by considering an unspecified number of possible antecedents. "Explanation," however, implies the existence of some definite rules or relationships, according to which certain observed events can reliably be said to have been caused by a set of specific antecedents. Finally, "prediction" (or, more appropriately, "inference") implies that a relationship is so well defined that an as yet unobserved effect can be inferred from observed antecedents. The three terms therefore are progressively more powerful in terms of their usefulness in the structure of science, as well as more exacting in terms of precision and evidence. Thus it can be argued that only the best explanations should lead to prediction. How can I demonstrate that I have satisfactorily explained a relationship, unless my explanation is in some way testable, precisely through the prediction, by deduction, of an event yet to be observed? Similarly, a confident assertion that anxiety about exams and Father's stern insistence upon lengthy study periods prompted Johnny's tantrum progresses from speculative "understanding" only when the relationships between these events are clearly *explained*, and these explanations tested by some *prediction*. "*Prediction*," by the way, does not necessarily imply that an event in the future must be involved. What matters is that the critical event is unknown at the time the prediction is made. The argument that archaeology cannot be a science because it deals only with events in the past, is therefore spurious. The archaeologist observes certain facts, and infers certain relationships which imply other events. If he then discovers evidence that such other events have indeed taken place, he has met the criteria of scientific inquiry.

It is important to insist upon this type of *inferential* prediction, for, as Toulmin (1953) observes, prediction may sometimes occur without understanding or explanation, as, for example, in the case of seasonal changes in ancient Egypt, simply by extrapolation from certain frequently observed regularities. "Prediction," as the term is used here, means therefore an inference about an as yet unobserved event, which may, but need not, have already occurred, and which is based upon an analysis of the relationships involved.

Science, to be exciting as a pursuit of knowledge, and useful toward furthering human well-being, need not be assumed to be a panacea. Although Hayek (1955, p. 14) criticizes the "exclusive claims" of science, the scientists who ascribe universal and unique benefits to science are not numerous. Most of them are too busy doing their work to go about preaching a gospel.

Scientific inquiry is not inimical to the everyday facts of life; it does not seek to subvert the useful knowledge which results from our daily experiences. Indeed, most scientific inquiries originate from everyday life. Everyday experience with fire led to a systematic investigation of the combustion process. Seasonal changes and their effects upon agriculture led to astronomy and meteorology. People fell ill and recovered or died, and it became advisable to study the variables affecting these events. People sometimes attack each other, at other times shake hands. It is not unreasonable to look systematically for relationship in that area also, even though we often predict quite successfully how another person will react to something we do. Science, then, is not at war with common sense. Rather, it systematically verifies, clarifies, and sometimes generalizes the statements which may have originated, however vaguely, in everyday observations. Sometimes, of course, it may show such a statement to be false.

Suppose, for instance, that we have been told that fat people are more sociable than thin people. Now, there might be several simple reasons for this state of affairs, in addition to some complex ones:

1. Fat people have some hereditary attribute which predisposes them to both obesity and sociability. They would continue to eat much even on a deserted island, and would continue to be sociable during a famine.

2. Fat people have some hereditary predisposition, but the two manifestations of eating and sociability only occur together. If one is suppressed, so is the other.

3. People who suffered hunger in childhood have a tendency to make up for their deprivation by eating a lot as adults. But since food deprivation often occurs together with a deprivation of love, they seek to compensate for this early lack also by being friendly, sociable, and merry.

4. People who were pampered as children with both attention and a great deal of food have learned to derive pleasure from both sources.

5. There is something in food, perhaps only in those foods which fat people predominantly eat, which increases sociability.

6. People who like company spend more time eating, and therefore eat more.

7. People who eat more spend more time at the table, and therefore have more time to socialize.

8. People who wish to ingratiate themselves with others do so in various ways; one of those is to accept hospitality, viz., food offerings.

9. Finally—although the list could no doubt be extended —we may find that we are misinformed. A careful tallying of "jolly" people among "fats" and "leans" may reveal that the "jollies" do not predominate at all among the "fats". How then did we, and many others, come to place so much faith in a false assertion? This can happen very easily through

what we might call selective perception and selective memory. We may acquire an item of information through hearsay, or by reading it somewhere, but once we "know" it, we sometimes tend to see and remember those events which confirm that belief in preference over events which would invalidate it.

It is, therefore, not surprising that on occasion science shows a plausible common belief to be wrong. For example we now know that the speed of free fall is not related to the weight of the falling body. But Galileo asked a question suggested by common experience, and his findings might just as easily have supported common beliefs. Furthermore, Galileo was not simply concerned with the truth or falsity of the belief. He also sought to express such relationships as "distance the body has fallen" and "speed of the body" in quantitative terms, again a step well beyond the imprecise assertion: "The higher the drop, the faster the speed". It is also true that as a science progresses, it may ask questions which are more recondite. From "What is the weight of a column of air at sea level?" inquiry may proceed to "what is the average molecular speed of a gas at a certain temperature?" These questions are by no means abstruse. First, the eventual usefulness of knowledge cannot be predicted (one need only think of Galvani's amusing, but totally useless "electrical" frog legs). Secondly, the minute inquiry often leads to a more accurate understanding of the large, obvious phenomenon. However abstruse the study of statics may have seemed at one time, no one would dream any longer of building a bridge relying upon common sense alone, or "a feeling" as to what strength the structure should have. Similarly, we now know that the threat of severe punishment is not the only or even the most effective deterrent from undesirable behavior, and that cramming is not the best way to study for an examination.

Thus, a venerable common sense belief may often give

incorrect information, but the crucial point is that we never find out whether such information is correct or not, since it is never put to a clear test.

HOW "OBJECTIVE" IS THE SCIENTIST?

The scientist endeavors to be absolutely objective in observing and recording facts or events. He will be very careful not to allow himself to perceive only those events which correspond to his expectation, at the expense of others. A person who believes that a dog's eating of grass predicts rain may pay attention and remember the times when the two events really followed each other (and perhaps even remember the number of such occurrences as being greater that it really was); the scientist, were he testing such a hypothesis, would keep a careful record of the dog's eating habits and the pattern of rainfall for the area. He would record all the instances when eating was not followed by rain and those of rainfall not preceded by grass eating. He would then engage in some fairly complex computations, not in order to browbeat the layman with his erudition, but to establish how often it might be expected to happen by chance that a dog's eating of grass might shortly thereafter be followed by rain. Only if the number of times this correspondence was actually observed exceeded this "chance frequency" by a certain amount, would he state that the relationship appears to exist, always allowing for the possibility that his inference might still be mistaken. After all, sometimes, though not often, you might toss a fair coin 10 times and get 10 heads. We shall look at some aspects of chance and probability in Chapter 5, for decisions based on such inferences are a basic aspect of the Scientific Method.

As a next step, the scientist would seek to find out why

such a peculiar relationship might hold. I have deliberately chosen an unlikely relationship in order to illustrate that even where an unsuspected covariation is observed, the scientist's task has only just begun. Chapter 4 will examine his subsequent steps.

But although scientists rightly insist that theirs is the objective way of acquiring knowledge, it can be seen from the foregoing that science, too, has its subjective aspects. The particular events to be observed in preference over others are clearly not dictated by nature, but the scientist's choice and his area of interest. Thus, three scientists might look at a diamond, and one might see it as an instrument of great hardness, the second as an object having certain optical properties, and the third (an economist) as an aging bachelor's best guarantee against loneliness. More important, the laws or relationships the scientist thinks up to account for the observed phenomena may be countered by those of another scientist, who has another explanation.

It is often thought that the scientist's task is simply the accumulation and arrangement of facts. Some scientists, unhappily, have encouraged this perception of themselves as mere recording devices of natural events.

The error of this definition becomes obvious when we consider that the scientist, like any other individual, is exposed, at every moment of his life, to an enormous number of stimuli or sensations. Some of these stimuli make an impact and are recorded by him; others, the great majority, simply occur unobserved. It is only a small step from here to the admission that not only is his "recording device" sensitive to some events, but not to others, but that he goes very far out of his way to expose himself to the kind of events that are of interest, and avoids others. The physicist during his working hours is to be found in his laboratory, and not in the pool parlor (although if he were hard pressed, he could probably make a reasonable case for his presence there, pointing to intriguing observations in the area of dynamics and thermo-dynamics). Moreover, we should find him in his laboratory not simply awaiting the occurrence of interesting events, but toiling persistently and ingeniously to produce conditions conducive to the occurrence of such events. He is experiment-ing, or doing research. This activity, so often cited, occa-sionally even by its perpetrators, in hushed tones reminiscent of secret devotional rites means, quite simply, that the scientist has, first of all, selected an area of interest, and arranged matters in a manner which he believes will lead to certain outcomes or events.

This activity consists, then, of more than a passive record-ing. It is only rarely, if ever, that discovery "discovers" the scientist; the story of the collision between an apple and Newton's head is apocryphal. Scientific discovery and knowl-edge comes only to the prepared, to those who have exposed themselves actively, usually for many years, to certain situations making the to-be-discovered event likely.

In this sense of choosing an area of investigation and even having certain hunches about what to look for, the scientist is, then, active indeed, as well as subjective. The thermometer measures temperature, the seismograph, earth tremors; similarly, one scientist might concentrate upon the composition of sugars, the other, upon thinking in rats (it appears that rats do think, though we cannot be sure about what, or exactly how). However, by preparing or observing special conditions which he thinks will produce certain events, the scientist has taken an indispensable further step. He has said, in effect: "I think that, if such and such a situation exists, such and such events will occur, affecting the object I am observing." He may, most certainly, be wrong, and sometimes the outcome of his experiment may be quite different. He may even conduct an investigation in order to find out which of a number of possible outcomes will happen, without having any definite opinions about any of them. But in each case the selective exposure to events described above constitutes, in fact, a hypothesis of some kind.

This initial hunch or hypothesis, it should be remembered, does not germinate in a vacuum. It is based upon prior observations and information. An early scientist may observe that water droplets appear on the outside of a cold glass of water in a warm room. His first hunch might be that the glass is porous, allowing water to seep through. But our scientist does not stop there. He tests his hunch: Is the glass really porous? If so, he ought to observe a gradual seeping through in all conditions, and the water collected on the outside added to that in the glass ought to add up to no more than the initial weight of the water in the glass. It is this testing of hunches or hypotheses which constitutes the dividing line between Scientific Inquiry and what we might call its cousin, Common Sense, and it is this difference which accounts for what is sometimes called the robustness of common sense, i.e., the longevity of most common sense beliefs, compared to scientific theories. From the cited examples it is apparent that common sense may or may not be right about its hunches, and that at the same time, it is often phrased so vaguely that its correctness cannot be established. A scientific hypothesis may be equally right or wrong, but it is the scientist's dissatisfaction with a flat, unproved assertion which makes it quite likely that his hypothesis will soon turn out to be wrong, while a similar common sense belief, being subject to no test, might endure for centuries. Eventually, however, our hypothetical researcher will formulate the current hypothesis about the water droplets, or, to be more precise, the hypothesis that under certain conditions condensation occurs, will be corroborated by experiments varying the differences in temperature between room and glass, and the humidity of the air in the room. But common sense cannot obtain this level of corroboration; the absence of a suitable test safeguards against a statement being proved wrong, but at the same time no way is available for choosing among various alternatives, all supported by pithy sayings.

The other reason for the robustness of common sense, and the fact that scientific statements are often rather unexciting to the layman and appear to deal with only a small segment of events, is that common sense deals ambitiously, but vaguely, with complex events, while science, at least in its early stages, examines relations among only a few variables, but attempts to do so with precision.

THE BASIC ASSUMPTIONS OF SCIENCE

After all that has been said about scientific rigor and objectivity, it may surprise some readers to learn that the scientist, too, has his articles of faith; he takes certain initial assumptions at face value. He will seek to make them plausible, and they must not, of course, contradict one another. But he does not attempt to prove them. Philosophically speaking, such a beginning is unavoidable. Whenever we make an assertion about something, we thereby assume that the words, or, more generally, the elements out of which our statement is composed, denote something; they have a certain meaning. We can carry our definition one step further and define our component terms, but the new definitions will again use terms which either have meanings we assume to be fixed and specified, or they must in turn be defined. It is not difficult to see that this process could be continued without end. Yet, we are able to converse freely, and most of the time understand one another, without endlessly having to define our terms. The secret, of course, is that we assume certain primitive terms, namely the basic vocabulary, grammar, and syntax of our language, and use them to express other meanings. Euclid's Geometry is an often cited example of an elaborate system of definitions and demonstrations using some very simple basic elements, so simple, in fact, that Euclid thought them to be "self-evident," and therefore not requiring proof.

Uniformity and permanence. The scientist assumes that the universe is uniform and permanent. This rather ponderous assertion means quite simply that, if a given relationship is discovered today in Denver, Colorado, the same relationship should exist tomorrow, in Tibet, and is presumed to have existed 3700 years ago, in Egypt. Take, for example, the relationship between time, acceleration, and distance: $S = 1/2 \ gt^2$. If the scientist discovers that the distance which an object falls in a vacuum varies slightly at various points on earth, he will not assume that the relationship itself changes with locale or time, and that for the top of Montblanc, $S = (say) \ .4999 \ gt^2$. If he thought that such relationships changed haphazardly through time and locale, then any attempt to understand—and even live in—the universe would be rather pointless. Instead, he will look for factors which would make his different results explainable within the framework of the assumed relationship. First, he might want to reassure himself that he has read his timepiece correctly, and that it is accurate. A replication of his findings by other scientists with other chronometers would settle that issue (you can see now why "replicability" is so important). Then, he might begin to suspect that g, the "constant" of acceleration, is constant only as the distance from the center of the earth remains constant, and since this is of course the answer, he will then very soon restate the relationship in such a way as to specify conditions for which g has the given value, and a new relation for g with regard to (or "as a function of") distance from the center of the earth.

The general assumption of uniformity and permanence is not violated when a theory is found to be inadequate, as was the case with the theory which assumed mutual attraction across a vacuum. The new theory which supersedes it—in this instance the Theory of Relativity—does not imply that the universe functioned according to one set of laws until Professor Einstein made his intricate calculations, and then changed abruptly. It means that certain new observations could not be explained in terms of the existing "laws," and that the newly formulated laws take into account and explain not only the new findings, but also the previous ones. A natural law is not, it must be remembered, a statement of what *should* be; it is simply a statement of a relationship among events. It therefore makes no sense to the scientist to speak of something happening "contrary to natural law." He must, if the entire concept of an orderly universe is not to collapse, assume that either a mistake has been made in the observation, or that the law, as heretofore stated, was inadequate to express the true state of affairs.

The world can be known.   This assertion, which appears a rather arrogant one at first sight, is again quite indispensable, if there is to be any kind of knowledge. As has been shown in Chapter 1, the origins and the "trustworthiness" of knowledge have worried philosophers since the days of ancient Greece. The scientist does not purport to have these ultimate answers, he simply proceeds "as if" it were possible for man to place some trust in the effectiveness of his perceptual and reasoning apparatus. If each time he saw a red apple, the scientist stopped to ask himself: "How do I know that everything I see and think is not a total figment of my mind?" or "How do I know that, when both of us look at what appears to me as a red apple, you, too, see the same thing (even though you *say* you do)?"* then there would be no sense in asking any further questions. In a way, by refusing to be paralyzed by these doubts, the scientist really applies "common sense," as you might, if you saw a truck bearing down upon you and leapt out of the way, without delaying to ask yourself whether the truck, the world, and you, are "really there."

The universe is determined.   This is the assertion which generates the greatest uneasiness, because it is often incorrectly seen as implying that everything behaves like an automaton, without spontaneity or originality. In our next chapter we shall examine some misapprehensions about the meaning of determination in the study of Man and the very real question about the usefulness of assuming absolute determinism under all conditions. For now, we shall be content to define the meaning and the more general implications of the term.

"Determinism" means that each event in the universe is completely given or defined by a finite number of other events in the universe. Therefore, if all these other events are known, the event under discussion can be completely deduced. The universe, in other words, contains no miracles in the sense that such an event would arise without being connected with other events.

Events do not occur without being caused.   Determinism in its philosophical sense does not imply causation. To say that two events are related is not the same as saying that one causes the other. In fact, Hume, in his Treatise on Human Nature, impressively questioned the whole concept of causality. He did concede, however, that it afforded comfort, and might have added that it made possible some under-

---

*The specific question of "private perceptions" will be explored further in Chapter 3.

standing of the universe. However naive it may have been of Dr. Johnson to kick a stone as a philosophical refutation of Hume's argument against causality, it was a beneficial kick for the scientist, without which he would once again find himself without questions, let alone answers.

We have called these basic assumptions "articles of faith," They really imply no mysterious system of beliefs. They are simply necessary in the pursuit of factual knowledge. In the words of Cohen (1953, p. 159), "By ruling out caprice, we rule out utter chaos."

WHAT IS A THEORY?

At a certain point, when some observations have been made, and some initial hunches tested, there may take place a process which is frequently misunderstood: The scientist may formulate a theory, say, about changes of liquids to gaseous states. What is such a theory? Is it ultimate and eternal truth? Why are so many theories disproved and discarded? Is it not likely that the same may soon happen to the particular theory with which we are concerned, and if so, why have a theory at all?

First of all, it must be admitted that some scientists think that we do not, in fact, need a theory—only collections of data. However, there are some very sound reasons why most scientists find theories useful, indeed indispensable, despite all the restrictions noted above.

1. A theory serves as a kind of condensation or summary of many related findings. Take the theory of gravitation again: It summarized and generalized in a few brief statements or formulae what happens to the pebble dropping from your hand, and to the earth revolving around the sun. Notice that the example given is an obsolete

theory, yet its usefulness is immediately obvious. This parsimony, or economy, first hinted at by Bishop Occam (Occam's Razor) and later formalized by Morgan (Morgan's Canon) simply asserts that, since there is no limit to the number of theories that can be devised to account satisfactorily for a system of relationships, the one containing the fewest assumptions is to be preferred. This very sensible requirement has been illustrated indirectly by Rube Goldberg, whose contraptions, it will be remembered, were the very antithesis of functional simplicity, and were humorous precisely because they utilized a large number of complex intervening devices in order to execute a trivial final task.

2. A theory is a statement of general relationships. In our instance of the condensation of water, it asserts relationships between temperature and air pressure on the one hand, and evaporation or condensation on the other.

3. As such a statement of relationships, a theory lays no claim to ultimate and everlasting truth. The sturdy and venerable theory of gravitation, thought to be unshakable, is no longer representative of our knowledge of mass, energy, space, and time.

4. Some theories are quite shortlived. The theory that characteristics which an organism inherits are transmitted through complex protein chains was soon superseded by the discovery of the properties of DNA and RNA. Indeed, a shortlived theory may sometimes be formulated by a scientist with the full expectation that it will soon be disproved. By stating precisely a network of relationships where no clear formulations had previously existed, he "forces" himself and his colleagues into purposeful research. This tactic is often used in a new science, such as psychology. It is for this reason that a brilliant scientist may state what may appear as rather unimpressive quantitative relationships between, say, hours of fasting and running speed to food. He has no delu-

sions about eternal and universal verities, but he has rephrased a vaguely stated relationship in researchable, testable terms, and made possible more precise and varied follow-ups.

5. It is, of course, not only possible, but extremely likely that our parsimonious law or theory may not express the true state of the world and that, in the words of Cohen (1953, p. 112) "Nature is more complicated than our simplest account of her, adequate as it may appear for a while." However, the scientist is not interested in one all-encompassing statement of nature. Such a statement would be necessarily vague. He is interested in optimally combining economy of (theoretical) explanation with the range encompassed by that explanation. The extremely parsimonious theory which accounts only for a very limited range of events is of little more value than a theory which, though it encompasses many diverse phenomena, is either so vaguely stated as to allow for no real "test," or contains so many variables that it represents no gain over the individual enumeration of the observed events. A theory is not a catalogue.

6. A theory is a predictor. It not only describes past events, but predicts future ones.

7. Theory, as I have indicated in 4, also channels further inquiry. Simply seeing a stone fall might have resulted in Galileo's studying, say, the various kinds of soil indented by the falling stone, if he had not had some very definite ideas about gravity which led him to think and experiment further along those lines.

From the above listed points it is obvious that no theory is of any value unless it is testable, or "falsifiable," This means that a theory must make its statements so as to lead to empirically observable predictions, and the predictions so observed must be stated precisely enough so that empirical evidence can either support the theory or disconfirm it. It should also be clear now why the scientist is seemingly cavalier when, at a cocktail party, somebody proposes to him a theory concerning the number of devils in Hell. They are hard to see, let alone count. In the words of Marx (1963), a theory is both a tool, enabling the scientist to look for further, still unconfirmed relationships, and a goal, in that it seeks to encompass, in a relatively small number of statements, discovered relationships among events. But just as scientific theories are not formulated capriciously, they also are not discarded or supplanted lightly. If the alteration and the modification of theories were matters of individual whim, then the scepticism and the derision of the enemies of science would be more than justified. One of the most important tasks of the scientist is to doubt and to question. But his is not the universal doubt of the dogmatic sceptic, who asserts that nothing can be known, nor the doubting derision of the dolt who does not distinguish between capricious and well documented statements, and seeks to assert his independence through arbitrary disbelief. The scientist doubts effectively and constructively, by proposing alternative viable explanations.

Science proceeds according to rather strict rules which are quite similar regardless of the topic of inquiry. These rules underlying the "game" of science are neither difficult to understand, nor implausible. Yet they have led to numerous misunderstandings by both scientists and opponents of the scientific method.

HOW THE "SCIENTIFIC GAME" IS PLAYED

1. Science must have its observable—or empirical—components; it rests on observation. We now understand why

psychology is often defined as the science of behavior, and not as the science of thought, soul, or mind. Behavior in its broadest sense — whether it is a reflex or the conduct of a person in high political office — *is observable*. Thoughts and emotions, except as they give rise to measurable physical events, are not observable. On the other hand, although some so-called radical empiricists do maintain that all knowledge is derived from sense impressions, this assertion does not mean that rational processes of ordering or thinking do not apply; for our purposes it is sufficient to assert that there can be no science based solely upon reflection, without the observation of any "real" events or facts.

2. Science is purposeful: It asks questions that are answerable in terms of observation or inference, and are relevant to the issue at hand.

3. Science is systematic: It tries to discover cause-effect relationships or events that predictably occur together in a consistent, repeatable manner.

4. From this it follows that, at least in principle, a scientific finding should be replicable, i.e., we should be able to obtain the same observation if we repeat the procedure and conditions exactly. I say this should be so "in principle," because not all observations occur in controlled experimental settings (sun eclipses, for instance, or economic depressions), yet they are legitimate objects of scientific inquiry.

Psychology too, as we shall see, avails itself of both the experimental and what we might call the "natural setting" methods.

5. Science is communicable. The inspirational insights of the mystic, the apodictic pronouncements of the charismatic leader, whatever their importance in the course of history, have no place in the edifice of science. If one scientist is able to obtain certain findings under certain conditions, these findings cannot be impressions, feelings, and stirrings within

him so intimate that "no one else could possibly know what he was talking about." It is this requirement that science be communicable which has given rise to the often criticized term "operationism" or "operationalism." It simply means that certain terms must be defined in order to make an assertion meaningful and the transmission of findings possible. This requirement may appear like tedious hairsplitting, until we consider how many different things even a commonly used term like "intelligence" may mean.

It is true that, in psychology especially, the indiscriminate and blind obeisance to operationalism had led to a good deal of nonsense. For instance, some people will maintain that "intelligence is what intelligence tests measure." This nonsensical "scientese" results from a confusion between a method of measuring, which is operationally defined, and the relation between that measure and many forms of behavior, such as, for instance, performance as measured by grade point average in college. This quite different "meaning," which *relates* two or more observable events, rather than simply stating what is *meant* by a term, could be called "factual meaning." In everyday parlance, operational meaning can be said to be the answer to the question: "What do you mean by your term?" The factual meaning is the empirically determined answer to the question: "How is this event or observation related to that one?" To this we might add a third meaning, which I shall call implied meaning, or the possible answers to the question—"What does this imply?" or, more simply, "So what?"

6. Science is self-correcting. By gradually eliminating errors it approximates more and more precise description, explanation, and prediction.

7. Finally, science is cumulative. This condition again follows from the preceding ones, and it is extremely im-

portant. The scientist of today does not have to rediscover the laws of gravitation or light refraction. Indeed, it is often observed quite rightly (though with vastly misleading implications) that the grammar school boy of today knows more about the nature of things than did Aristotle or Galen. This is not so much to the credit of the schoolboy, as to that of the rules of the game of science. The poet or the painter of today competes with Shakespeare and Michelangelo in terms of his own ability. Despite some refinements of techniques nothing others have done before him adds to his fund of skills. The kindergarten genius freely expressing himself in blots of paint or attempts at poetry does not stand upon the shoulders of past titans. Science, on the other hand, requires its Newtons and Einsteins for giant steps, but once these steps have been taken, they are part of the permanent repertory of humanity, and progress toward further knowledge can be continued through the work of lesser lights.

All this shows not that the scientist always speaks only about solidly demonstrated facts, and never permits himself to have hunches or intuitions. On the contrary, the truly creative scientist is unthinkable without them. But, he clearly separates proved findings from speculations yet to be demonstrated, and his speculations will be so phrased as to be susceptible to empirical test.

DEDUCTION VS. INDUCTION

Most of us have become accustomed to drawing a sharp line between the deductive process and that of induction. The first is represented by the situation where a specific statement follows from general ones by a logical process, while induction proceeds from specific instances to generalities or "universals." However, as Cohen (1953, p. 115) points out, no "true" induction is possible in the empirical sciences (as opposed to such purely logical structures as mathematics). At least one of the premisses involved in induction must be specific. For instance, the inductively derived law of gravity is inevitably bound to particular and specific local conditions, such as, for instance, the exact value of g. Strict deduction, on the other hand, requires that the deduced statement follow by implication from the premisses, as in a mathematical or logical proof, or that the premisses contain all possible observable cases, which is clearly impossible.

In a simple but elegant model, Amsel (1965, pp. 187 ff) demonstrates how deduction and induction develop in the empirical sciences: Think of one of those children's puzzles in which numbered points are joined to form the outline of, say, a chicken. Now for each point substitute an event or an experimental finding, and for the entire chicken, substitute the relationship, law, or theory, which ties them together. In out instance, the law is:

> "Begin at the numeral '1' and draw a straight line to the numeral '2', then proceed to '3', and so forth, until the largest numeral is reached."

Clearly, by having points, facts, or events, and the order in which they are connected, the relationship or theory is already given and the chicken becomes readily visible after the purely mechanical task of connecting them is completed.

Then, Amsel says:

> "Now let us change the game a bit. The page is now, not a scattering of isolated dots with numerals next to them, but a page almost black with dots. Only some of these dots outline the pattern which is hidden, and there are no numerals at all to guide the joining of these critical points. But you still have to find the hidden animal, by joining dots. You don't know how many dots to join, or where they are on the page. Your task is complicated by the fact that in order to outline the hidden animal you must first find the points in the total complex of points that are relevant (have a number) and then find what number each point has."

In other words, we have a page containing not only the meaningful dots but many other irrelevant ones, and there are no numbers to indicate which are part of the design, and the order in which they should be connected. Your task is still to find the "meaningful" points (or experimental findings), those whose outline produces the hidden design, and to connect them properly. If we assume that each point or finding is shown to be "meaningful" if it contains a relevant variable, some aspect which has some bearing upon the general issue under examination, then, by proceeding systematically, say, from left to right, line by line, we can gradually classify each point as either meaningful or meaningless. Examining all possible events and extracting the relevant ones showing meaningful interrelationships is equivalent to discovering a system of relationships inductively. But since, as has been pointed out earlier, it is impossible to observe "all possible" events or "relevant points," because their number is obviously infinite, the question then reduces to *when*, in the process of observing events, you formulate your first hypothesis, or when, at a given moment in the "chicken" game, you say to yourself, "This is beginning to look like a chicken; if it is, then this specific point, and that one, should be 'meaningful' and 'relevant,'" you are applying deduction. You are stating a tentative hypothesis and testing it; keeping in mind that what looked like the beginnings of a chicken to you might have looked like portions of a wrist watch to someone else, and that his subsequent hypothesis might also be corroborated by other relevant points, or appropriately designed tests. There is no limit to the number of theories that can account for a finite number of observations.

It is also obvious that the guessing game will in every likelihood lead to some unproductive guesses, so that the inductive process of systematic scanning will have to be resumed. The important point is that there is no uniquely valid cut-off point at which induction must end or deduction begin. The continuous processes of theory formation, theory testing, and occasional theory rejection are based upon an unceasing interplay of observations related to inductive and deductive reasoning.

Finally, it should be clear that trying to guess the hidden figure without connecting any lines at all, i.e., without conducting empirical tests, is quite pointless. Arguing again by analogy: Pure speculation, i.e., a hypothesis without any observation, without assaying any parts in the puzzle, is clearly of no value toward an understanding of what events are relevant, and how they are related.

THE ISSUE OF REDUCTIONISM

Reductionism is the explanation of one class of phenomena through the relations expressed by another, more basic class. The most basic class of phenomena is usually—though not necessarily—considered to be physics. Thus, to explain changes in temperature purely in terms of molecular movements, i.e., physical correlates, would be an instance of reductionism. The fact that all observable phenomena are necessarily physical has led to much misunderstanding, since this has been taken by many laymen—and by some scientists—to mean that all events are "nothing but" the movements of atoms and electrons.

However, as Nagel (1961, p. 282) points out, reductionism is not a necessary assumption for the scientific method, and it is not implied by determinism. Nor does determinism imply that all events are physical or mechanical in nature. A mechanistic system predicts only mechanical events. Molecular movements and position at a given point in time determine some subsequent movements and positions, but predict nothing about other, nonmechanical phenomena accompanying those subsequent mechanical states. To give a simple example, nothing in the chemical properties of oxygen and hydrogen allows us to predict the chemical properties of water, simply because the descriptive system makes no assertion about the properties of water as, say, a solvent. But then, deterministic prediction does not mean that we should be able to deduce all the chemical, optical, physical, and other characteristics of a compound from a description of individual components. We have a precisely stated relationship among such variables as the quantities of individual components entering into the compound, conditions of purity, temperature, and pressure under which fusion occurs, *et cetera.* Any "irregularity" in a predicted relationship no matter how complex, has to be fully explainable in terms of previously unsuspected variables, if the theory predicting the relationship is to stand. But it is not properties, but events which are determined. Properties themselves can be predicted only when the system of relationships, the *theory*, contains statements which connect not only events, but properties. Thus, the various properties of water such as clearness, thirst-quenching, *et cetera,* could be predicted if various statements about light propagation, solvents, and solutions were incorporated into the original theory stating the conditions under which oxygen and hydrogen combine to form water.

This somewhat lengthy chapter has attempted to present a picture of science in general, but emphasizes the exact and inanimate sciences. The following chapter examines the scientific study of the so-called behavioral sciences, and specifically psychology, i.e., the ways in which human and other organisms function and act in their environment.

CHAPTER 3

The Scientific Study of Human Behavior

In the preceding chapter I have presented the ground rules for the scientific method. But the practices of the scientist are by no means universally favored. There are obscurantists who either profess complete disinterest in factual knowledge, doubt that any worthwhile factual knowledge can be obtained, or place their trust in extranatural agencies through magical invocations and exhortations. The use of magic, as has been pointed out, does not imply that the efforts expended necessarily lead to failure. The scientist may sometimes find the witch doctor's practices far more successful than his own. The difference between magical and scientific method lies in the degree to which relationships are tested and explained; if a raindancer were consistently successful in "producing" rain, the scientist would expect to find a natural explanation for the raindancer's success (this is not as farfetched as it seems; the raindancer might merely be an accurate weather forecaster, and dance only at very promising times).

It may seem rather pointless to build up an elaborate case about the fantastic aberrations produced by magical thinking. After all, few of us still indulge in rain dances, and even though we may throw a pinch of salt over our left shoulder after spilling it, and avoid walking under a ladder, we do so somewhat with tongue in cheek. A bridge is built not where a sheep's entrails suggest, but at a location optimal from economic, demographic, and topographic viewpoints. The very primitive winds of superstition are no longer "in."

However, some of what Esper (1964, p. 242) calls "irrational shots in the dark" have assumed the guise of modern rigor and sophistication. Psychoanalytic theory, existentialist psychology, and depth psychology have all the trappings of 20th century terminology, but their structure and methods are so vague as to allow for so many inferences—often contradictory among themselves—as to preclude any kind of derived inference, and thus any test of their assertions.* This does not mean, of course, that their statements are always completely and categorically wrong, but that, since there seldom is a way to test their assertions against observations, we can rarely know how closely these assertions correspond to facts.

It is rather suprising that a large number of people who are wholly committed to the application of science to inanimate objects, nurture either a deep fear or complete scepticism about the scientist's ability to study the behavior of organisms, especially that of Man. (In passing, it should be pointed out that even behavioral scientists are not always free from such misgivings, especially in their leisure time.) As Handy (1964) so soberly puts it: "Without in any way overstating the already available results of scientific inquiry into the problems of men in society, the widespread conviction that these problems either are not amenable to scien-

---

*In the last decade or so, ingenious attempts have been made to translate psychoanalytic concepts into testable hypotheses, sometimes with seeming success. What must be kept in mind here is the important distinction between observable events and hypothesized underlying structures. We can, for instance, derive a prediction of "repression under stress" from an infinite number of assumptions about the causes of this phenomenon, but we have no way to connect this prediction to such constructs as "ego" or "id."

tific study or that short-cut remedies can be substituted for that study, may be the chief hurdles to be overcome." (p. 81)

Perhaps it is merely painful to renounce the unlimited power one has for so long attributed to oneself, and to have to admit that one is necessarily affected by past and present external events. Further, the sceptical position, somewhat absurdly, occurs quite often in conjunction with the alarmist view, which fears the behavioral scientist because of his present or potential accomplishments. This is a particularly unfortunate form of obscurantism, because in some instances it is advocated by eminent persons in the so-called exact sciences, and thus acquires all the more weight in the minds of the public. Yet, some reflection shows that such a position is just as dogmatic as that of the fortunately rare behavioral evangelist, who asserts with apodictic certainty that his methods will reveal all that is worth knowing about Man. For what this special type of obscurantist is really saying is:

1. Nothing important about Man can be known through scientific inquiry; or

2. The scientific method can indeed learn something about why organisms, including people, behave in certain ways, but that this knowledge would be ignoble and demeaning to both knower and known.

As to the first point, the evidence against it is simply overwhelming. Over the last 80 years or so, the sheer bulk of our accumulated knowledge about how people (or animals) learn, see, behave in various special situations such as stress, and think, fills many volumes. It is irrelevant to reproach the psychologist with having failed to predict A's suicide or B's fame and eminence attained in spite of tremendous odds. The physicist's exactitude also occurs only in absolutely controlled laboratory conditions; he would have little success in predicting the directions in which a handful of pebbles dropped from my hand would bounce after they strike the floor. Similarly, the variables with which the behavioral scientist must deal in a "real-life" situation are many; yet, as in the case of the physicist, the search for basic relationships is not rendered useless for that reason. We do not, nor shall we ever know everything, but our present knowledge is immensely greater than it ever was.

The second point, which expresses fear of knowledge, deserves more careful consideration. I shall return to it later in this chapter, after a closer look at this popular monster, behavioral science in general, and psychology in particular.

IS SCIENTIFIC PSYCHOLOGY REDUCTIONISTIC?

Even though we have dealt with the more general aspects of reductionism in the previous chapter, we might do well to examine the issue in the particular context of psychology. The term can be interpreted in three ways, none of which, as will be demonstrated, follows from the premisses or methods of the behavioral scientist.

Scientific knowledge about human behavior is criticized because of three alleged implications:

1. Man is "nothing but" an animal; his occasional brilliance and nobility differ from animal behaviors only in quantity, not in quality.

2. The behavior of living organisms, including man, is "nothing but" the mechanical motion of nuclear particles.

3. Man is "nothing but" a bundle of needs and drives, such as hunger, fear, and sex.

Before answering these points individually, it is important to distinguish "reduction" from "parsimony." We have already seen that a scientist in any field must, if an infinity of possible theories is to be avoided, state his relationships in the most economical manner possible. This requirement does not imply, however, that all theories must be simple, or that, because some events in a given category or class are explainable in terms of a simple theory, all events in that class must be amenable to explanation by that same theory. Whether they are or not is quite obviously a matter for the empirical testing of hypotheses.

The rebuttals to the three forms of reductionism imputed to psychology follow easily:

1. There is ample evidence that some human functions closely resemble those of some animals, especially higher-order mammals. This is not surprising, in view of the many similarities in their anatomical and physiological structures. It would be just as fallacious to argue that therefore all human behaviors have their counterparts in animals, as that there can be no similarity of any kind between animal and man.

2. The notion of "emergence" has already been discussed in the previous chapter. To recapitulate very briefly: Not only does determinism have nothing to say about the properties of water as deducible from the properties of hydrogen and oxygen, but the premises of the scientific method do not imply that the emotions and thoughts of living organisms are reducible to mechanical events in the organism. Mechanical determinism applies to mechanical events only. Even though it makes precise predictions about the movement of billiard balls, it says nothing about their color. If a prediction about color is to be made, antecedents of color, such as pigmentation, light, and perceptual properties of the observer, must be given. An analogous argument applies to human thoughts or emotions, which are assumed to be determined, but for whose prediction extremely complex antecedent information is required. This

information, among many other things, might include previous thoughts, physiological state, and perceptual factors.

3. The extent to which human behavior can be accounted for in terms of rather primitive or basic needs is, once more, a proper topic for inquiry, not pontification. Certainly nothing in the rulebook asserts that all human motives are aimed at maintaining the basic functions of survival. Parsimony implies that such a simple explanation, where applicable, is to be preferred to a more complex one, but says nothing about the breadth of applicability of such a simple theory. The question is not: "Do some recondite, complex processes take place?" but: "Are we, by assuming elaborate processes, able to understand, explain, and predict behaviors of varying complexity better than with a simple theory?" This may often be the case. The impossibility of defining all behavior in, say, physiological terms becomes obvious when we consider that most of the time behavior is social, i.e., it occurs between organisms, and therefore its description and explanation must contain terms other than those of physiology.

Thus, emotion as expressed verbally or otherwise may or may not be accompanied by precisely measurable physiological events. Both may be of interest, but this renders the two sets of observations no more equivalent than the optical and the mechanical properties of a diamond. To cite a further example, given by Mandler and Kessen (1959, pp. 264 ff), a table has functional uses quite independent from its chemical or physical characteristics. The function of motivated behavior is similarly distinct from its physical (or physiological) attributes.

We might note in passing that the obverse of our first example of reductionism sometimes leads to the absurd kind of anthropomorphizing exemplified by S. Carragher's "Wild Heritage" (1965), as well as by the highly respected

Washburn in her "Animal Mind" (1936). Both authors attribute to some animals, endowed with only modest status on the evolutionary scale, highly complex thoughts and emotions.

When a scientist refuses to be content with the speculation that the human life was God's creation, he does so not because he is necessarily a confirmed atheist, but because to do so is an abandonment of the scientific quest. If a refusal to abandon such a quest, to continue to seek answers is arrogant, then the refusal to acquiesce in war, disease, hunger, and premature death as being divinely ordained, is by definition presumptuous. Yet, without in any way minimizing the suffering and the horrors of today, would this world be a nobler place if the Black Death continued to rage through the world, unchecked by arrogant question-asking scientists?

DOES KNOWLEDGE IMPLY INTERVENTION?

Muddled thinking by the self-appointed defenders of Man's integrity often confuses knowledge with intervention, although it is not hard to see that knowing something about a relationship does not imply that one must then intervene to change it. However, to the student of behavior, the choice *not* to intervene is more plausible when it is an informed rather than an uninformed choice. Moreover, those who admonish against "tampering" with nature very often do just that, from ignorance and with disastrous results.

Thus, the mantle of the villainous scientist has been placed on the shoulders of the behavioral scientist, and one might, if one were so inclined, speculate about the ready glee with which some scholars in other fields, only recently rescued from the popular image of cruel, mad, or at least weird scientists, have seconded this change with loudly voiced indignation about the behavioral scientist who so confidently and presumptuously asserts that human behavior can be studied, and, as if this indignity were not enough, presumes to draw some inferences from such animals as chimpanzees, cats, even the simple-witted pigeon and the unglamorous rat.

DETERMINISM AND THE STATURE OF MAN

It is clear that the decision to assume that, a) the universe exists and b) that we can know something about it, already contains the seeds of determinism. This logical step has been taken with few qualms by the exact scientists, and in those areas has become generally accepted. Leaving aside the more complex notion of strict causality, determinism asserts simply that events are fully determined or specified by other, observable events. The assumption of determinism does not exclude probabilistic statements, and is not negated by Heisenberg's misnamed indeterminacy principle. The assumption (and it is just that) of even probabilistic determinism, and the additional one that events have at least probabilistic causes, however, have aroused considerable anxiety when applied to human behavior. Free will and human dignity are seen as being attacked on several fronts:

1. All life is allegedly reduced to a narrow, mechanistic explanation.

2. Determinism reduces the properties of a complex event to those of its components.

3. Man is a will-less object, moved here and there by external forces acting upon him.

4. Man is coerced into actions.

5. Determinism limits the scope of human variety.

6. Determinism implies atheism.

Let us see whether any of these alleged consequences follow from an assumption of determinism:

1. The assumption of determinism does not imply a reduction of all phenomena to their physical or physiological correlates. To say that an event, in order to be scientifically meaningful, must have physical correlates is not the same as saying that it is "nothing but" those physical events. Such an assertion would be as absurd as asserting that, since there can be no fever without a change in a thermometer reading, fever is "nothing but" an expansion of a column of mercury.

2. Determinism makes no assertion about a complex event in terms of its components. As has been shown, the attributes of water cannot be inferred from those of oxygen and hydrogen, nor can a diamond be predicted deductively from carbon and certain long-range physical forces acting upon it. These "emergent" properties, even in the relatively simple examples here cited, are ascertainable only by observation, not deductive inference. This does not mean, of course, that the scientist will not carefully study the variables affecting the union of oxygen and hydrogen or the precise physical and chemical events producing a diamond.

3. Determinism does not assert either that man is willless, or that the forces acting upon him are solely external. It does assert that even such complex concepts as human values and motives can be studied scientifically and systematically. Since there is nothing in the assumption of determinism which implies that an organism is affected only by environmental events, the amply demonstrated findings that eye color and, to a large degree intelligence, are hereditary pose no problem for deterministic explanations.

4. Determinism does not imply that a person finds himself coerced or pushed into doing something against which "his very being" revolts. The argument runs quite dif-

ferently. Our values and knowledge of right and wrong are determined by our being human, 20th Century Americans, perhaps having been raised according to a certain faith, and so on. When faced with a choice, these values should then make us want to do the "right thing," or select one class of anticipated outcomes over another. Indeed, our whole educational process, religious and secular, is based upon the fundamental premise that subsequent choices will be affected by such teachings. (Even a totally unfettered or "permissive" approach, such as that practised at Summerhill, is not contradictory to the deterministic assumption; it merely assumes that the determinants of choices, i.e., ethical values, are part of the natural equipment of man.) The choice of outcomes may range from committing multiple murder to heroic self-sacrifice. Our behaviors, then, are seen as *responsible* in the sense that such a choice is made, but they are not indeterminate, chaotic, or capricious, and are assumed to be at present largely unpredictable because many of the variables involved are obscure. However, we aim at such prediction in our daily interactions with others, as well as within the larger scope of international relations. We wish to produce, in the stranger we encounter on a lonely street at night, the choice *not* to attack us, and even to perceive such an attack as utterly unacceptable. All of us attempt to predict and manipulate human behavior most of the time, are pleased, though little surprised, when we succeed, and shocked when we fail. We seek to sway and predict others for the most exalted reasons, such as compassion, love, and altruism. If I seek to understand another person's reasons or motives for acting in a certain manner, am I thereby lessening his stature? Would it not, instead, be far more derogatory to arrive at the consensus that there are no discoverable, "reasonable" grounds for his behavior? Our moral training is therefore not in contradiction with, but utterly dependent upon the assumptions of determinism and (practical) causality. It is hoped that through such training a person will learn to know right from wrong, and act accordingly.

When we apply a moral judgment to a specific decision by a man, we do so on the basis of two considerations: a) Was he able to apply his ethical repertory, or was the present situation such that no knowledge could conceivably be of any value to him, so that he had to choose randomly from his behavioral repertory? Surely, no credit belongs to him in the latter event, even though the results may be fortuitously beneficial, while the former clearly implies that his choice was the deliberate product of his assessment of the present situation in terms of his value system, and thus is subject to moral judgment. b) Was he able to predict to some extent how his choice would affect the world? If not, his choice is again ethically meaningless and totally solipsistic. Any prediction of the effects of one's action, however, again implies that the other person's feelings and actions will at least to some extent be affected — determined — by one's acts. Thus, I have a "free choice," or an opportunity to commit murder, but being what I am, the product of my particular experiences (which may include not only high moral values, but the learned expectation that murderers often suffer painful consequences of their acts), I refrain from the crime. The *determinants* of my lawful, even virtuous behavior, may range from sheer self-interest to the very noblest of motives. Further, my act (or, in the given instance, my non-act) is capable of moral evaluation only if, in addition to my ability to assess the act itself, it is also assumed that I had some expectation as to how my behavior would affect others (for example, the prospective victims). Without this additional clause, which asserts not only that my values and motives (and hence my actions) are determined, but also that I perceive my own behavior as a determinant of other events, moral judgment becomes again pointless; for what is the moral value of anything I do or do not do, if I have no expectation at all as to how it will affect the world? It is, incidentally, at this crucial point that the existentialist maxim of "acting responsibly" falls short. There can be no responsibility without some expectations, and there can be no expectations without assuming determinism and causality. Further, the substance of this argument is not affected, whether we think of "strict" causality (A causes B), or "probabilistic" causality (A increases the likelihood of B).

Determinism is therefore not only compatible with human dignity and conscience, it is indispensable to it. It assumes that the individual is an orderly and, at least in theory, predictable product of his past and his "nature." Whatever he does, wishes, or fears is the outcome of his past experiences, whether they were observable to others or not, and yes, his hereditary and congenital characteristics. Conversely, a person whose nature and behavior change—or rather, are changed—in a totally capricious manner, is thereby reduced to a straw in the wind, however benevolent that wind. Seeming caprice and unpredictability are present in the defective airplane wing, the flight of the swallow, and frequently the behavior of child and man. The two former are ethically inferior, not superior, to man (and, we hope, child) because they cannot learn the difference between right and wrong, and govern their behaviors accordingly.

5. The assumption of determinism does not set a limit to variability. Williams James asserted that it would never be possible to write an individual's biography in advance. This can now be logically demonstrated. Chomsky (1957) has shown that it is possible, using a finite number of English words, to form an infinite number of grammatically correct and quite sensible sentences. (One way of performing this

amusing trick is to insert relative clauses ad infinitum, like this: 1. The man smiled; 2. The man wearing the grey hat smiled; 3. The man wearing the grey hat he had just bought smiled; *etc., etc.*) Since the number of sentences describing actual states of the world is also infinite, a correspondingly infinite number of events can "determine" a person's behavior or personality. This realization does not, of course, invalidate behavioral prediction, it merely makes it probabilistic; instead of an event being strictly determined by a finite number of other events, approximations become progressively more accurate as more variables become known.

6. As to the question of God, determinism does not imply atheism, not even, in fact, a remote deism. Divine intervention itself, however, would have to be presumed as occurring in such a manner as to be in some way related to the existing state of the world. A "miracle," in the sense of a highly improbable event, can occur. An utterly capricious one, which upsets the orderliness of nature, cannot. This assumption need not imply lack of omnipotence, but simply a kind of orderliness and consistency. It assumes that God does not play dice with the world. Admittedly, if even a "miraculous" event has at least some small probability of occurring, and can be explained solely in terms of natural causes, God's intervention and existence can never be proved. But this is an old dilemma. Nothing about the extra- or supranatural can be proved or disproved by empirical methods. The scientist who stubbornly looks for the natural causes of an apparent miracle is not necessarily an atheist; his inquiry does not, and cannot, answer questions concerning final causes, only immediate ones. God may exist for the scientist, but not as an all powerful, completely capricious Child-God.

IS DETERMINISM ABSOLUTE?

There has been much speculation and fruitless debate among philosophers, but also among scientists in various fields, as to whether determinism can be proved or disproved. Only lately Chein (1965) and Immerglueck (1964) debated the hoary issue. The American philosopher, Scriven, who earlier (1956) could not prove that human behavior is in principle undetermined, later (1966) argues for indeterminacy as follows: Imagine that one individual C thinks (rightly or wrongly) that another person P seeks to predict his, C's, behavior. C can always, if he so chooses, select a different behavior to make P's prediction false.

This very telling argument does not, however, provide a final answer. It assumes, first of all, that C's interest in proving P wrong always overrules any other interest; it further assumes that C is aware of P's prediction, and finally, it assumes infinite processing capacity, "taking account of alternatives," for, though C may also outwit a third party, Q, who observes how C is "fooling" P, and attempts in his turn to predict what C will do, there may be a fourth person observing the other three, and a fifth, and so on.

These arguments are, of course, quite academic. The simple fact of the matter is that not only the behavioral scientist, but almost everyone assumes that the feelings, beliefs, and behavior of others are the result of certain conditions, hereditary or environmental; in other words, that the sum total of what a person is and what has happened to him will affect what he does.

Ultimately, both determinism and indeterminism are assumptions. The difference between the two is that the assumption of determinism not only in inanimate nature or the lower forms of life, but also in Man, makes it possible to function in what would otherwise be complete social chaos.

The question is not: "Is it true that every event in every man's life is 'truly' determined?" but "Can we, by assuming determinism, not only predict the response of the stranger whom we ask for information but also attain a cumulative and systematic understanding of what makes people behave in certain ways?"

THE OTHER PERSON: HOW CAN WE KNOW HIM?

The old epistemological problem of how "mind" can understand "matter" continues to be rediscovered by eager critics. The implication drawn by the early psychologists, and by some even to this day, is that we must earnestly and systematically look into ourselves, "introspect," in order to discover the elements of our sensations, feelings, and cognitions. But Gorgias' insoluble dilemma continues to haunt them: Individual introspectors arrived at different elements, at different times. Each person, in other words, experiences differently, and not necessarily with any degree of consistency. Experience, knowledge, feelings are unavoidably subjective and, since words themselves "mean" different things over time, and for different individuals, we have come to the end of the *cul de sac* proposed by Gorgias: "If anything could be known, it could not be communicated."

The absurdities inherent in the phenomenological position go further: Why love, if we can never know how the other person is affected and responds? Why have moral or ethical standards, if their effects can never be known? After all, our own perception of having done something worthy may have no relationship to fact. Why bother to enter into polemics with imaginary opponents existing only in one's own mind, even though they may be arguing that they, and I, and the world, really exist?

The deadlock allows for two choices: We either resign ourselves to knowing nothing about others and ourselves (hunches, insights, and intuitions may *lead* to systematic, communicable knowledge, but only after they are properly verified and stated in public terms), or we must use what there is in terms of "data" or "facts" to conduct our study as best we can.

Certain rear-guard actions have attempted to preserve the bridge between the ineffable and the knowable. Some existential psychologists seek to resolve the insoluble dilemma by means of a subterfuge: Though the other person's experiences are strictly private and cannot be communicated by means of observable behaviors, the skilled and empathic observer can infer them by intensely imagining himself in the other person's position.

Hayek (1955, pp. 25 ff), too, seeks the best of the two possible worlds of naturalism and phenomenology. He concedes that other people often react to situations as we ourselves would—if there were not this basic stratum of "comparability," no human action at all would be possible, and we would live in utter chaos. But, proceeds Hayck, it is also undeniable that people often perceive events in different ways, even though these events seem the same to us, and, conversely, perceive similarities among seemingly disparate events. Such perceptions are inexplicable in objective or naturalistic terms, and can be understood only if we find out what went on in the minds of these perceivers, what were their bases for perceiving those events.

There are several rather obvious difficulties with this line of thought. First of all, it seems reasonable in cases like this to look for additional aspects in the stimulus situations which could have been overlooked or overemphasized by some perceiver and produced the stated differences. Secondly, it is now common knowledge that past experiences influence the perception of an event in the present. A person who has once imbibed a very dry martini on the top of Mount Everest may perceive a connection between those two objects which would be totally incomprehensible to others. But this does not mean that the only, or even the safest way to explain such idiosyncratic perceptions is to ask the perceiver the reasons for his unique perception. The events leading to it are clearly amenable to objective study; moreover, the person himself may not even be able to recall the significant events, so that we are once more faced with the seemingly unavoidable task of relating private events such as individually unique perceptions to public, commonly observable ones.

Third, and most important: For the sake of argument, let us concede Hayek's arbitrary dichotomy that a person exhibits two neatly separable kinds of behavior, those explainable in terms of observable events, and those for which no objectively verifiable antecedents are possible. The crucial question now becomes once more: Where is the dividing line? Unless I have searched carefully for observable antecedents, how can I be sure that there are none? In other words, unless Hayek's position included also a universally applicable statement as to where objective inquiry must stop—and this is clearly impossible since conditions differ for every person and event—even his scepticism does not preclude inquiry.

Finally, if one wanted to press the point, one might even wonder how any type of knowledge, whether it had been gained through observation or intuition, can become more than, once more, an incommunicable property of the person now studying the other, unless he, in turn, phrases it, and commits it to the record, so that others can avail themselves of his discoveries.

Royce (1959, p. 521) remarks that "The existential criterion of knowledge accepts as true that which ultimately enhances man's existence or being, and rejects as false that which diminishes his being." This statement unintentionally pinpoints an insoluble dilemma: If there is to be no external criterion or public validation of "enhancement," would Hitler, Caligula, Schweitzer, and Gandhi have to be considered as having attained equally exalted levels of self-fulfilment and "truth"?

These viewpoints, then, are the unfortunate outcome of a serious logical fallacy. When I try to understand the other person's feelings or emotions, this implies three steps:

1. I make an inference about certain similarities based upon other, *observed* similarities, e.g., he is human, and so am I, hence we must have something in common.

2. I consequently infer that when he experiences certain events, he will react to them in a manner somewhat similar to the way in which I should react, were I to experience these same events; his fears and hopes in a certain situation will be comparable to mine.

3. I seek to verify my inferences.

Why do we believe that a stone has no thoughts, feelings, or emotions? Because there are no points of similarity or analogy between it and us. It follows that the empathic inference is impossible without observation; observation, moreover, which usually entails more than simply noting the other person's human form. I either leap to the conclusion, or must gather prior evidence, that he is indeed "comparable" to me. Then, unless I have additional specific evidence that a certain stimulus has impinged upon him, has been registered, all my conjectures regarding his inner experiences become pointless: He may not have noticed or understood the stimulus situation at all!

But this is not all. Having made my very subtle conjectures, I must now seek evidence, however slight, that I have done so with some degree of accuracy, otherwise I am once more engaged in a totally solipsistic process. My speculation may be *totally wrong*. Thus, even the empathic inference must rely upon observation both *before* and *after* its occurrence.

The scientist, to sum up, does not deny the supreme importance of your "inner life" for yourself. He simply argues that what matters to others, even those who love you dearly, is the totality of your behavior, i.e., everything they can observe about you. This, not because they do not care about what goes on inside of you, but because the only possible clues they can have about such inner events are the expressions you give to them.

This viewpoint is shared by some existentialists and behavioral scientists, but the consequences they draw differ radically. The existentialist assumes that your inferences about the other person are accurate, if achieved under conditions of "empathy," or placing yourself into the other person's position. The psychologist, though he frequently must also depend upon inferences, formulates them in the form of hypotheses or theories, and tests the predictions he derives. This inference and verification about the feelings, beliefs, and emotions of others are entirely legitimate (though some argue, not indispensable) endeavors, provided they are anchored in observational variables. Some reflection also shows that these steps are followed whenever we attempt to understand even the most intense and noble emotions. To amplify somewhat James' (1890) concept of the "mechanical sweetheart," the feeling of my beloved toward me are meaningful only in that I am able to infer them from certain observable events. I assume, first, that my affection will engender in her the same response I should offer if affection were offered me. This inference is based upon previous observed affinities, otherwise it is, after all, possible that she might respond to my devotion with indifference or worse. Then, I again verify my observation: Does she love me? If she does, then she should say certain things, or act in a certain way. In other words, having made my inference, I make a prediction. The dear lady's inner feelings, if they are totally unsupported by any observable event whatsoever, or perhaps even contradicted by it, have no meaning for me.

James proposes a "mechanical bride" (shades of McLuhan), in order to show, by reductio ad absurdum, that even a replica imitating every conceivable behavior would not be the equivalent of a living person, and Cohen (1953, p. 316) defends James' assertion that the existence of consciousness is proved by the patent absurdity of such a bride. Consciousness, he argues, is a trait, and a trait by definition makes a difference; also, since we can detect degrees of "soulfulness" in people, its total absence in a robot must be all the more detectable. This argument, however, simply begs the question: It assumes that consciousness is a thing, separable from other characteristics, and that "soulfulness" is a quality independent of behaviors and not inferred from them, so that no suitable behaviors could be programmed into our robot. Both assertions are clearly arbitrary; we could study the precise observations which lead to the inference of "soulfulness," and program them into the robot. Indeed, if a limited degree of "unpredictability" is one of the attributes of bridal soulfulness, such a random process is obviously also amenable to duplication.

Most of us, most of the time, seek to "predict" the behavior of others, sometimes for the noblest reasons. Indeed, as I have argued, none of my social actions has any moral meaning unless, a) I have the ability to make a considered choice, and b) I have some idea of the effects of my action upon the other person. We should keep in mind here that this position does not preclude "introspection," in the sense of a person's statements about what he experiences, as important observable data. It merely argues that such reports cannot be taken as the only and final truth, if there is to be a scientific study of Man. It is also not maintained that every such inner experience must be translatable into words, as long as it results in some observable event which I, as the observer, can code and record.

How can we judge the accuracy of introspection? Only 1. by comparing it to other observations on that organism; 2. by equating antecedent events and applying them to a similar organism (say, ourselves). For instance, the figural after-effect is a rather startling phenomenon in perception. Under appropriate conditions, staring fixedly at a drawing produces a weakened image, both in terms of contrast and density of the individual lines of the drawing. This is a completely "internal" event for the observer. What makes it amenable to systematic scientific inquiry is the fact that the experience is quite general, that it can be communicated with relative ease, and that systematic variations of the effect can be produced.

Compare with this subjective event instances of complex emotions, of mixed feelings. Their direct expression is hampered by their variability for different people, and even for a given person over time. Add to this the incontrovertible evidence that sometimes people do not even know what "moves" them, and that often another person is a better judge of "inner states" than its possessor, and the indispensability of observation should become obvious. Even if I can make a reasonable inference that your feelings, when bumping into a stone, are similar to mine, no matter how well you disguise them, I must still be able to *describe* them to myself and others, have a protocol of them, in order that they might form part of a common body of knowledge. It will not do at all to argue: "But if you have understood my feelings, what need is there to describe them?" Someone else, observing your mishap, may experience a completely different "understanding." Empathic understanding is, thus, a probabilistic inference originating from observable events, and resulting in the prediction of other observable events. And in fact, if we observe an alien organism, e.g., a person from a totally different culture, we assume less similarity and our inferences and predictions are more restrained, even though that person may be exposed to quite common situations and may even emit superficially similar gestures. Yet, unless there is observed comparability, we profess little knowledge about the person's inner state.

Our study, then, must deal with observable facts which, of course, may include not only movements, but speech, sighs, changes in facial expression, etc. When we move from speculation to observable events, we are simply taking the same inevitable steps that liberated other fields of knowledge from fruitless metaphysical meanderings. Not only the effects of stress upon a bridge or light upon a photographic film, but also the diet of a diabetic and the characteristics of a learning or perception require observation, the formulation of hypotheses, their testing, the communication of findings to others, and the ability of those others to reproduce the findings.

THE GOAL OF THE SCIENTIFIC EXAMINATION OF BEHAVIOR: ESTHETIC DELIGHT OR ACCURATE EXPLANATION?

But how, a layman or even a (non-behavioral) scientist might ask can such a procedure tell us anything worthwhile about Man? Granting even that a man will behave in a roughly predictable manner when his knee is tapped or when you tickle the soles of his feet, granting even that you can make certain uninteresting predictions about somewhat more complex situations such as hunger, fear, or fatigue, of what use is this information in determining the "essence" of a man, his courage, his devotion, his persistence in the face of adversity, the joy of his companionship?

Much has been made of the prosaic descriptions and explanations which arise out of science, as opposed to the esthetic power of the artist, poet, or writer. The implied corollary of these arguments is, once more, that science deals with only trivial aspects of life, and that the great insights must come from other sources. But it is not the degree of knowledge that differentiates the great scientist from the great writer, but the type of knowledge, and its purpose. An artist (the term is to be understood in the general sense, as a person pursuing any one of the arts) need not deal with people. His concerns may be rocks, music, scents, and so forth. Whatever the subject matter of his work, his aims and methods, and therefore the kind of communication he provides, differ completely from those of the scientist. The poet praising the formation of certain rocks is only minimally interested in their origin and development. The geologist does not have their esthetic attributes as his primary concern. Dostoievsky, describing the complexities of father-son and brother-to-brother relationships, has given us delights and insights which are perhaps unequalled in their impact upon our intuitive understanding of unique instances of human actions and conflicts. But before we would base decisions for other situations involving families and crimes, we would probably want to know more about what general relationships are involved, and how certain differences between our situation and that of the Karamazovs might lead to different predicted outcomes. Artistic knowledge, then, provides us with pleasures and knowledge for which science certainly can offer no substitute. On the other hand, the general relationships or laws discovered by systematic inquiry, whether they deal with rock formations or human behavior, are not superseded by the poet's genius. As Broadbent (1961) puts it, even the most effective method of producing saints is subject to empirical investigation (p. 46).

A hematologist, studying certain properties of that mysterious, life-carrying liquid, blood, does not reject its mechanical similarities with other liquids, he uses them to determine how blood circulates, and how blood pressure varies. Our critics are not appalled at similarities between their digestive or reproductive systems and those of dogs or even rats. Yet, even those similarities are sufficient to entail at least some behavioral similarities between man and beast. Hayek's argument that mind cannot study itself may be an ingenious puzzler, but it just is not true, nor do the opponents of a scientific study of Man generally assert it. Professor Hayek, too, studies his mind, and self-observation and self-correction can even be programmed into a computer.

In other words, it makes no sense to assert beforehand that "we cannot know." The scientist, much more cautiously, might argue that we do not know whether it is possible to know, and that the only way to find out is to keep looking!

There is, as I have said, nothing in the scientific investigation of human behavior which asserts that all behavior is simple. If it were, then the scientist could confidently make predictions about complex human events, instead of laying himself open to derision and outrage over the simpler relationships he often studies. If the many kinds of behaviors and attitudes which define a successful college student are more complex than those which prompt him to doodle on a piece of paper in a moment of boredom, then, clearly, a very complex set of laws or statements is needed. As pointed out earlier, one need not insist that *all* the determinants of such complex activities be within the scope of enumeration and rigorous definition. But after all if our predictions can become *more* precise as we continue to ask questions, without even becoming *absolutely* precise, gains in knowledge have been made. Does this mean that the behavioral scientist asks for carte blanche to speculate indefinitely on complex human behavior without any evidence that he is on the right track? Not at all; for the validity of his method of inquiry is borne out by the gradually improving approximations he achieves in his predictions. That we have learned some fairly good rules about human behavior through such inquiry can hardly be questioned. The advertising industry, though not necessarily a glorious example, is at least a convincing one.

As we have seen, then, the behavioral scientist does not assert that a person's inner experiences are either nonexistent or irrelevant. Motivation and personality, conflicts and decision behavior are major areas of psychological inquiry. He does not deny that I may experience emotions and ideas that are so fleeting—or so complex—that I cannot begin to make them evident to him. He simply argues that unless and until I can make my experiences available to him to some degree, they cannot in any way affect his knowledge, feelings, or behavior, and, a fortiori, cannot form part of the public body of systematic knowledge known as science.

It is possible, however, to go one step beyond and assert, in fact, that one's own inner experiences are inchoate and meaningless until they are in some way observed by oneself. How do we decide whether we are happy or moody, passionately in love, or the sudden recipients of a brilliant cosmic insight? First, we state to ourselves, subvocally or by means of imagined gestures, certain inner states. We hold a dialogue with ourselves, however rudimentary or habitual. Having stated to ourselves what we think or feel, we then compare our present state with our own past states, or the inferred states of others. In other words, not only the minds of others, but our own mind becomes known to us only when translated into behavior, however subtle or complex. This exploration of self involves skill, intelligence, and rigor, and it is really not surprising that many people do not know themselves as well as others might know them. Such current phrases as: "I didn't know what to think," or "I don't know what I am going to do next," attest to this, by no means uncommon phenomenon.

HOW CAN WE KNOW THAT WHICH HAS NOT BEEN EXPERIENCED?

This is a frequently offered argument against the scientific study of people: In order to "know" a certain emotion, you have to have experienced it. Therefore, description without the concomitant experience is of no value to the person to whom it is described; on the other hand, if he has experienced the emotion, explanation is redundant. Thus, Hume argued that a mild man could form no idea of cruelty or revenge. However, defining an experience does not mean recreating or duplicating it, and explaining how different emotions are produced is not equivalent to describing how they feel.

The argument confuses participation with description. The pathologist is interested in describing the physiological effects of a malignant growth while the psychologist might be intested in the effects of such a growth upon a person's behavior and attitudes (such effects may arise directly, through the physiological changes caused in the patient, or indirectly, through his knowledge or belief that he is ill). Neither the psychologist nor the pathologist claim to know "what it is like" to be so afflicted; they try to understand and explain relationships between an abnormal growth on the one hand, and physiological and psychological changes on the other. The latter may be actions or statements, but they must be something which the observer can "put his finger on," can record and transmit, and which other, similarly qualified observers, can repeat.

Now, it might be argued further that the effects of such a horrible event are not properly assessed by these clumsy devices. The patient's whole outlook on life changes, he experiences previously unknown states of agony, perhaps religious conversion, or an enormous resentment against the rest of the universe. He may write a poem or a novel, though he previously had shown no such talent. Those about him, his family, his friends, are also affected emotionally and perhaps economically. Does the scientist really expect to understand, explain, and predict all this with his trivial probings, so devoid of sympathy and "understanding" (in the emphatic sense of the word)?

Is it true that I can know about others only by knowing what I myself have experienced? If this means that a motive must be conceivable to the scientist, as must be a positive electron, this position is no doubt correct, but it is also meaningless, because being conceivable does not imply existence, and, more important, does not imply existence in a given individual under examination. To illustrate the more general case, we can readily conceive of an element with an atomic weight of 1700, but presumably such an element does not exist.

For the second argument, even though the motive to destroy one's children is conceivable to me, and may even have been demonstrated for a given person, this tells me nothing about another individual in whom I am interested at this moment.

The answers given above may still not preclude the accusation by the inspired sceptic that, whatever knowledge is gained by these methods is certainly trivial. Yet the accusation of triviality can be turned around. Is it more trivial to say that: "Repeated task failures produced a lowering in productivity," than: "He realized his utter worthlessness and just gave up"?

The latter statement admittedly sounds more impressive, but upon close inspection really tells us very little. It is the former which specifies precisely what events led to a very intersting change in a person's behavior, and allows us to investigate systematically, for instance, the relation between degree of failure and loss of productivity.

IS IGNORANCE PREFERABLE?

Let us look, then, at those who, like Krutch (1956) dread the scientific study of Man, and argue that it is preferable to preserve a certain mystery about human nature. It is better not to know, especially if the knowledge one anticipates might greatly impair the stature of Man.

It has always seemed to me that this argument, far from defining its proponent as a person with a deep respect for humanity, and the behavioral scientist as a callow Peeping Tom, really exposes the former as having very little confidence in, if not the perfection, then at least the perfectibility of Man. The behavioral scientist, on the other hand, starts with the fundamental assumption that human behavior is modifiable, and therefore improvable.

What are the fruits of ignorance? Without even offering the striking instances where pestilences as well as ethnic and social discriminations have been at least to some degree corrected through knowledge about microorganisms on the one hand, and factors in human learning on the other, is ignorance about the needs, fears, and motives, in sum, the raising of a child, preferable to knowledge? Is the sexual ignorance described so vividly by Ellis (1954, p. 214) to be preferred to knowing? Not everyone might agree immediately that such ignorance is to be deplored, but in all likelihood those who would still cling to that position after it has been made explicit would be only a small nucleus of all those who, without having thought through the implications of their argument, make vague noises of horror whenever some relationship between an antecedent and a consequent event in human affairs is asserted. And yet, more knowledge affords more, not less, choice.

And if, in the last analysis, the growing understanding of human behavior might conceivably lead to unwarranted manipulations, interferences, and degradation, the answer to this possibility lies not in burying one's head in the sand, but in taking a hand toward directing such knowledge toward an enhancement of Man's destiny. I leave it to the reader to judge whether such efforts would be more effective if originating from an informed as opposed to an ignorant source. We have already examined the general distrust of knowledge, or, more precisely, of intellect. Little remains to be added except, perhaps, a statement of my own position, though the possessive pronoun implies no claim to originality.

I do not accept the pseudo-logical argument that, since a man concerned only with intellect and scientific knowledge may be admittedly an impoverished human being, a man can therefore experience a full measure of feeling only if he is uncontaminated by intellectual endeavors.

I am not ready to concede that men (or cultures) are destined for decline and eventual oblivion when they outgrow their beliefs in myths and magic. Their acts and thoughts are no longer influenced by the carrot of ultimate reward, nor muddled by the thoughtlessness which often masquerades as emotion. The creations of Shakespeare, Homer, Sophocles, and Nietzsche have neither the pollyannish optimism of the religious or ideological faithful, nor the dumb awe of the primitive. Are they therefore decadent, inferior to those of believers like Tolstoy, Dostoievski, and Milton? The cold light of intellect is cold only because it does not allow itself to float in a cloud of hot air. It is not new either in the history of Man, or that of Western culture. Periodically, the spurious arguments of vague romantic passion and blind, unreasoning faith become transparent, and men no longer fear the loss of humanity through the use of reason. Perhaps such a time has come once again.

CHAPTER 4

On Doing Research

DEFINING ONE'S TERMS

We have now come to the point where we might wish to examine some of the ways in which the behavioral scientist obtains his information. "Information" here, as we already know, means not simply isolated facts, except perhaps at the very earliest stage of development for a given science. The cataloguing of plants and animals undertaken by Linnaeus was, we now know, a necessary preamble to the science of biology, but it would be inadequate by itself to establish biology as a science. Scientific knowledge is a knowledge of relationships, and it is with such relationships that the behavioral scientist is concerned. He may initially be interested in the mere classification of people into categories of "anxious" or "calm"; that is, he will define some observable actions and classify them in this manner. He may define a given behavior or action in any way he chooses, by a mathematical symbol, an expressly coined word, or a word already in common use, as long as he employs this definition consistently. For instance, if he is interested in the relationship between light intensity and reading speed, he may call the first "x" and the second "y," or he may give them imaginary names, and then go on to state the relationship (obviously one which first increases, then decreases; it is difficult to read with minimal or very intense lighting). In fact, this is what the physicist does when he speaks of the relationship between, say, the emission of alpha particles and changes in nuclear structure. This is possible because neither is part of the everyday experience of most of us, and no names have been given to them.

The psychologist is in a somewhat different position. He deals with aspects of nature which are to a considerable degree part of our daily lives. We speak of "anxiety," "calm," "aggressiveness," "intelligence," and other attributes, but we seldom bother to define precisely what we mean by such terms. The physicist on occasion has a similar problem, for instance when he uses "energy" in a very precise sense, but such definitions are usually so clearly distinct from common usage of these terms that little confusion results.

This state of affairs imposes a peculiar burden upon the student of behavior. He may examine behaviors which have some components related to commonly observed attributes, and may use terms from the English language. But if he calls certain observed behaviors "anxious," he runs the very obvious risk of implying, for each and every reader, characteristics which that particular reader associates with his own, very personal idea of "anxiety," but which may be quite unrelated to the scientist's observation. Here, the importance of defining one's terms, first examined in Chapter 2, becomes obvious.

These difficulties of communicating accurately also explain why it is common for behavioral scientists to coin new terms for their concepts. This often engenders irritation and derision in the layman. However, the scientist who calls helpfulness "nurturance" is not necessarily being pompous; he simply tries, not always elegantly or with maximal success, to communicate a concept based upon precisely defined observations, and to avoid the many implications and subjective meanings inherent in more commonly used, though seemingly equivalent expressions. As was pointed out earlier, the scientist rarely deals with problems unrelated to previous observation, and in the behavioral sciences, these observations may be the same behaviors one encounters every day. Thus, he might observe or learn from others that, when people are prevented from attaining a certain goal, they are irritable, may engage in patently pointless behaviors, or attack another person. The expression that one usually hears ascribed to this syndrome is "frustration," and indeed some psychologists use that term to describe the general inner state of a person in such a situation. Others, however, use the term "frustration" to define the act of thwarting, or interposing obstacles, as exemplified by the phrase: "He frustrates me," meaning that he interferes with me, or does not allow me to have my way. These two uses of the term "frustration," both quite popular, are entirely distinct. One refers to an inner state supposedly experienced by a person, the other, to some observable actions performed by one person (the frustrator) in relation to another. It is clear that the scientist cannot permit himself the looseness of nomenclature which may be quite acceptable in everyday life (although there, too, it often leads to serious misunderstandings). He has two alternatives; in the particular example cited he must either use the term "frustration" in one of its two meanings, defining it in a seemingly pedestrian fashion, and use another term for its other meaning, or he may choose two entirely new terms for the two meanings of "frustration." This latter tactic may appear pedantic and sometimes brings to the English language terms that are neither mellifluous nor intuitively obvious, but it has the advantage of avoiding confusion when the scientist makes a statement. His first obligation, then, is to be entirely clear and unambiguous in the use of his terms. Simple as its substance is, the scientist's insistence upon such definition constitutes a giant step in the direction of precise communication: Describe the observable events which completely define the term you are using! In our instance, "interference with the goal-directed activity of another," might be an acceptable definition of this kind. (Although we observe that at least one term in our definition, viz., "goal-directed," might, itself, require definition.)

This "operational" definition or meaning eliminates much needless confusion. The scientist, in seeking a relationship between some experience imposed upon an organism and its response to that experience, will now rarely say: "I frightened it," or "I or "I made it anxious". Instead, he will precisely define the *operations* or technique he used to present a given stimulus to the organism. The effects of such a practice upon clarity in communication and the replication of one scientist's study by another are immediately obvious. One form of meaning is, then, the operational definition of a term; a statement of what the term *means*.

There come to mind two questions, both of which, happily, lead us to a second kind of meaning or definition of a term.

WHAT IS INSIDE THE ORGANISM?

Question No. 1. raised by a convenient and intelligent interlocutor, might run about as follows:

"You have mentioned a fair sample of names describing what I have always been accustomed to consider the very essence of a man's—or, for that matter, a higher animal's—'inner life.' Do you really mean to say that it makes no sense to speak of a man being afraid, or angry, or frustrated, except by defining these inner states by the stimuli we impose upon him, the things we do to him? Is there, then, nothing we can know, surmise, or even care about what goes on 'inside,' or do you go even beyond that and hold that even the most complex living organism is just a bundle of simple reflexes?"

Question No. 2. "Let us assume that you find a very precise relationship between something you do to the organism, a stimulus, and something it does thereupon, a response. You have argued passionately against those who say that *no* generalizations at all are possible; this, you say, is a matter for empirical investigation, not dogmatic assertion. Yet such generalizations, at least at seemingly obvious levels, are always made. When you keep a rat without food for 4 hours and then observe the speed with which it gobbles its food, you may display commendable caution about generalizing about the relationship between length of fasting and speed of eating in a teenager, but you will have no hesitation at all to predict that the same, or a similar rat will again display somewhat *similar* eating behavior following somewhat *similar* deprivation. Presumably, you will not be too concerned if the deprivation period this time is three hours and 59 minutes, or four hours and 1 1/2 minutes.

"Yet, even this seemingly quite plausible and certainly modest generalization is impossible if you view the situation solely in terms of a stimulus and a response, for as soon as you speak of *similar*, rather than absolutely *identical*, situations, you are making the very important implication that the stimulus in some orderly way affects or changes the organism, and that it is this change in the organism which determines its response, rather than some simple, rigid connection between a stimulus and a response."

Both points are quite correct and have, in fact, formed the two-pronged weapon whereby philosophy of science has invalidated the basic conceptual behaviorism of John Watson.

First, we have already seen that the modern psychologist does not for a moment believe that there is nothing inside the organism. He only asks that these inner states stand in some orderly relationship to antecedent and consequent observable events. The term "hunger" is readily admissible, even though nobody has ever observed "hunger," but only inferred it from observed eating behavior, or from the duration of the organism's fast. "Hunger" here is assumed to vary in an orderly way with time of deprivation on the one hand, and to affect eating in a similarly orderly fashion on the other, like this:

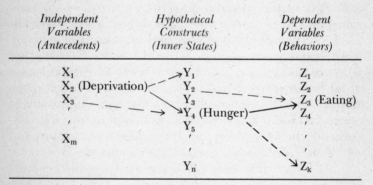

This model is quite flexible; it asserts that deprivation produces states other than "hunger," and that hunger may be produced by antecedents other than deprivation; also, hunger leads to behaviors other than eating, and eating may be produced by inner states other than hunger.

But note that our intangible concept of "hunger"—psychologists call it a "hypothetical construct"—is more precisely defined than, say, "anxiety," because we can make some fairly precise predictions as to how various stimulus situations such as deprivation, or the injection of glucose into the bloodstream, affect eating, presumably by changing the internal "hunger" state in an orderly fashion. (The fact that after extreme deprivation the organism may be dead, or so weak as to be unable to eat, is irrelevant; it is sufficient if we can produce a limited range of situations where the relationship holds.) With "anxiety," though it is potentially an extremely useful construct, our hypothesized state is far less clear. What stimulus variable produces orderly changes in it even over a limited range, and what behaviors are the orderly results of such changes?

Thus, we are not free to conjure up just any magical inner state; this would clearly lead to a completely useless proliferation of meaningless terms. The hypothetical construct, though by definition not observable, must stand in an orderly relationship to both antecedent (stimulus) and consequent (response) variables.

It takes only one further step to realize that the assumption of such constructs is not only convenient and intuitively plausible, but logically indispensable if we wish to engage in even the modest kind of generalization, or rather extrapolation, from observed relationships to unobserved ones having some degree of similarity. Now it makes sense to say that longer deprivation produces more eating, because such deprivation is assumed to change the organism's inner state in a certain way, a change which we have chosen to call "hunger," and eating behavior is directly determined by this state.

Our second type of definition, then, proceeds not in terms of the events themselves defining a term, but rather in terms of orderly relationships between events on the one hand, and hypothesized inner states on the other.

If we now return to our example of ambiguous usage, we see that the two ways in which the term "frustration" is often used are precisely those of operational definition and hypothetical construct, respectively. When we define "frustration" as thwarting or interfering with goal-directed behavior, we have defined the term operationally. When we consider the inner state presumably experienced by someone under certain conditions, we are introducing the hypothetical construct "frustration," and must carefully relate this state to conditions which cause it, and to observable behaviors which it presumably engenders.

SYMBOLIZING A RELATIONSHIP

Scientists look for relationships, or the manner in which at least two types of events are related, rather than for isolated facts or data. This does not mean, however, that all relationships are of scientific interest. For instance, since we arbitrarily call the quantity of 16 ounces a "pound," it is of relatively little interest to reiterate that the relationship of

"pounds" to ounces equals $\dfrac{\text{number of ounces}}{16}$. This is a log-

ical, or a *priori* relation; the scientist looks for empirical relations, occurring among *events*. Yet this relationship meets the mathematical requirements of a "relation" or a "function" (we need not concern ourselves with the distinction between these two terms). We can state it as above, or we can represent it as a table giving some values for ounces and the corresponding values for pounds:

ounces	pounds
1	1/16
8	1/2
16	1
etc.	

It is obvious that no matter how many values we list in this manner, we never can list them all, so that we must rely upon the intuition of the reader to realize that the general relation: "ounces = $\dfrac{\text{pounds}}{16}$", is involved, and not just a number of specific values.

Finally, we can represent the relationship on a graph consisting of a pair of "coordinates" like this:

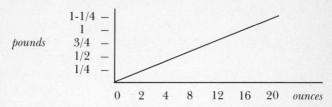

The spacing used for the values assigned is obviously quite arbitrary, as long as it is consistent. We could just as validly present the relationship like this:

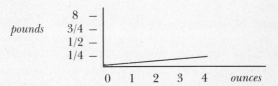

This initially confusing property of graphs is often mis-used to convey erroneous impressions to the unwary, who tend to derive more optimistic or, as the case might be, alarmist feelings from a steeply rising line than from a gently ascending one.

By convention, the vertical axis, the "ordinate" is used to express the "derived" value, or that which expresses something in terms of some original value, while the horizontal axis, the "abscissa," is used to show the original values. In our instance, since we are expressing pounds in terms of ounces, pounds are plotted on the ordinate. We could, of course, just as easily define ounces in terms of pounds, thus: "ounces = 16 × pounds"; this expression would then be plotted by placing ounces on the ordinate, and pounds on the abscissa. The values plotted on the ordinate make up what is also called the *dependent* variable, while those on the abscissa constitute the *independent* variable. The example illustrates, however, a very important point: a relationship and its mathematical or functional representation imply nothing whatever about *causality*: pounds do not cause ounces, nor ounces pounds. We can, of course, easily think of a causal relationship so represented: for instance, the number of words remembered as determined by, or "as a function of" the number of times the list of words has been seen. In these instances, the variable under study, here the amount remembered, is always plotted on the ordinate. It is, obviously, the dependent variable, since it *depends*, in this instance causally, upon the amount of practice. But if we keep in mind that a relationship, however stated, does not *necessarily* imply that the independent variable "causes" the dependent variable, then we shall easily avoid the all-too-frequent pitfall of reading extravagant significance into some graphic representations.

THE MEANING OF A RELATIONSHIP

It must now be admitted that the scientist, though he looks for empirical relationships, will very soon, as knowledge of his subject matter increases, be dissatisfied with relationships, however striking, which allow of no causal interpretation. Let us assume, for instance, (and quite fictitiously) that a relation is found between amount of nailbiting and gregariousness: the greater the amount of nailbiting, the more the person seeks out the company of others. This may be quite an interesting discovery, especially if it is confirmed by repeated observations making it unlikely that we are dealing with a fluke of chance. But very soon the obvious question must be asked: "Why this quaint relationship? Does nailbiting cause a person to be more desirous of being with other people? Does being with others engender nailbiting? or, finally, is there a common, underlying factor which affects both a person's gregariousness and his tendency to bite his nails?"

Clearly, no matter how often we observe the relationship, we can learn nothing from such observations of a mere mathematical "correlation" that would allow us to answer these questions. The only way to answer them is to observe changes in one of the two variables clearly preceding in time any changes in the other. For instance, if we curtail nailbiting opportunites and observe subsequent drops in gregariousness, and by forcing Tom to bite his nails more we observe him in a mad pursuit of any possible companion, then we have prima facie evidence that nailbiting, at least indirectly, affects gregariousness. If, moreover, the obverse effects do not hold, i.e., if, by forcing Tom to associate with people to a greater or lesser degree, no changes in nailbiting are observed, we can exclude gregariousness as a cause of nailbiting. More likely, however, we might discover that neither causes the other and that some third variable, perhaps changes in the person's economic or familial affairs affects both nailbiting *and* a craving for the company of others.

It is for this reason that statements of relationships, some of which are initially quite promising, soon lose interest unless some causal ties are established, and it is for this same reason that the scientist, wherever possible, collects his information through experiments, rather than through the mere observation in nature of occurrences varying in correspondence. Clearly, if a change in A affects B, but a change in B does nothing to A, we know more than by knowing simply that A and B vary together.

Incidentally, a relationship, causal or otherwise, need not be perfect to be of value; indeed it may be quite small, and still be immensely important, by the mere fact of its existence. For instance, a certain vaccine may reduce the incidence of a disease from 10% to 8%. Not everybody who receives the vaccine remains free from the disease, and not everyone who is not vaccinated contracts it; but the difference in the proportions, if it is consistent and therefore unlikely to be just an accidental finding, is clearly important. We shall examine the ways by which we decide whether a finding is or is not likely to have occurred by chance in the next chapter.

ERRORS AND CONTROLS

Suppose we wish to test the effects of a vaccine upon a particular disease. We could simply give the vaccine to one person, and observe whether he later becomes ill. But this does not constitute a very effective experiment. The man may become ill anyway, yet others might have been helped; the vaccine may be effective without being so in every case. On the other hand, if he remains healthy, we do not really know whether he would have contracted the disease if he had not been vaccinated.

Another possible experiment is to administer the vaccine to a number of individuals. At first sight this appears like a foolproof method, for we now have observations over many people, rather than just one. Previously, a similar group developed the disease in 10% of the cases, while our group shows an incidence of only 8%. But the matter is not that simple. It is quite possible that the results may not be due to the independent variable, the vaccine, at all, but to some quite extraneous and unsuspected circumstance. For instance, the present group may obtain better nourishment, may be subjected to less air pollution, may take more (or less) physical exercise, and so on ad infinitum. In order to be reasonably confident that seemingly positive findings are due to the variable of interest, and not to something quite different, we must also have a group called a "control group," which is similar to our vaccinated group in as many respects as possible, and differs only in the fact that it does not receive the vaccine. It is of course true that we can never hope to eliminate, or "control for" *all* possible differences; their number is infinite; but the scientist tries to control for some factors that would quite obviously confuse the issue. Some of these factors consist of differences in the subjects making up the two groups; for instance, the members of the vaccinated group may generally be healthier, or younger, or come from a different part of the country, and so forth. This factor of *subject* differences is controlled by assigning individuals randomly to the various conditions from a large pool of subjects, and thereby minimizing the likelihood of systematic differences among groups, or—this is often preferable—by matching the two groups on all the seemingly relevant subject characteristics. Some of these characteristics may, in subsequent studies, be found to have no importance; conversely, a new variable, not considered previously, may later be found to account for the observed difference between the groups which had previously been ascribed to the effects of the vaccine. The most spectacular of these factors, which was soon found to be present in many experimental situations, is the placebo effect. In our instance, the differences between the two groups might be due not to the vaccine itself, but to the fact that the experimental subjects were treated, while the control subjects were not. The effect here might be due to some form of autosuggestion, or to the puncturing of the skin when the vaccination was performed. Both of these possibilities can be tested by giving to some subjects vaccinations consisting only of an inert liquid, without so informing them. If the difference between this group and the one actually receiving the vaccine again occurs, it cannot be due to autosuggestion; if the placebo group does not differ from subjects receiving no vaccination at all, the "trauma" effect can also be discounted.

It should be very clear by now why carefully controlled experiments are necessary, even though this sometimes results in some individuals — the control subjects — not receiving what *later* proves to be a beneficial, even lifesaving, treatment. Unless this seemingly callous step is taken, it is often not possible to decide whether the effects of the treatment are genuine or spurious.

Another source of error must occasionally be controlled: in studies where the effects of an experimental treatment are less unambiguous than the presence or absence of a clearly defined disease, it may happen that the experimenter *thinks* he perceives differences between his experimental and his control subjects, usually favoring his hypothesis. This distorted perception is rarely fraudulent; not only does the average scientist value his life's work too much, but usually experiments of some importance are replicated sooner or later, and he would soon find himself exposed, if not as a fraud, then at least as a bungler. However, scientists — as it might not be remiss to point out once more — are human, subject to error, and a large body of psychological findings shows that such errors of perception occur preponderantly in the direction of one's hopes and expectations. There is, of course, a simple way out of that problem: have someone else administer the vaccinations, so that the scientist making his observations on a given subject does not know whether vaccine or placebo was administered. (In addition, the observations themselves might also be made by an outside observer, who neither knows nor cares what effects are predicted, and thus can record the data more dispassionately.)

There are, then, sources of error against which we can and should safeguard by appropriate experimental design. They are called "constant" errors, and once we have progressed beyond a very naive stage in developing scientific ways of thought, they are quite easy to understand.

Errors which are little more puzzling are the so-called "random" errors. Given the unavoidable fact that we can make only a finite number of observations with, it is hoped, a considerable but nonetheless finite degree of accuracy, using instruments which may approach, but can never reach perfection, it is inevitable that, say, the chronometer used to measure reaction time fluctuates in its accuracy by some tiny amount. Even the seemingly constant yardstick varies ever so slightly over time. Of course, the person reading the instrument or observing the events also varies over time in the manner in which he observes and records. The subjects, too, and the environmental setting can only approximate, or fluctuate about, some ideally existing average. When we say a person is 69.52 inches tall, we may base this statement upon one measurement. When measuring him again, a minute later, we may obtain a reading of 69.51 inches; then 69.54 inches, and so forth. The fluctuations may be due to fluctuations in the subject, the yardstick, or the way we read it. It seems advisable to use more than one measurement, and compute an average of some sort; this does indeed reduce the magnitude of random errors and in this instance, the more measurements we take, the more the computed average will approach the person's "true" height. But since we neither wish nor are able to continue our measurements into infinity, this "true" value can only be approached, but not reached, and a cut-off point for our measuring procedure is set, beyond which the cost of additional accuracy is considered to exceed its value.

It so happens that our techniques of measuring the height of people are accurate enough so that very rarely is the additional accuracy obtained by making more than one measurement worth the trouble; but the only slightly less obvious example of heart rate illustrates the point. Although two heartbeats should suffice to compute heart rate, a physician usually counts for 30 seconds or even a minute to compensate for fluctuations in the heart beat itself, and in the reading of his time piece. (In this instance the unavoidable irregularities in the watch itself are too small to matter.)

It is important to remember that these random fluctuations are not the systematic errors due to, say, a subject's growth over time (he may grow a little even in one minute), the effects of breathing upon heart rate, differences in calibration between two seemingly identical measuring devices, or consistent differences in perceptual acuity or reaction time due to, for instance, the observer's progressive fatigue. These belong in the category of errors controllable by experimental design, while the only way to minimize the effects of random errors lies in making them so small in comparison to the experimental effects that, in effect, they cease to matter.

CHAPTER 5
Measurement and Precision

At the beginning of every academic year I receive a visit from one or more prospective psychology students whose interest in psychology is readily seen to be, at best, lukewarm. The interview which ensues never fails to leave me troubled. For what these poor students seek is not so much training in psychology, as escape from some other science, reputed to be more exact and therefore, alas, to place greater demands upon mathematical ability. I should be a hypocrite were I to conceal that the alacrity with which I disabuse these hopeful young people is partly engendered by a degree of resentment that psychology should be so widely viewed as a "soft" science, i.e., one largely devoid of quantification. The result is, however, a highly dependable predictor of the prospective student's future: Those who are not frightened away by my warnings are quite likely to do well. (Unfortunately, I cannot establish whether psychology also loses some good prospects.) For psychology, as it is taught at all the major universities today, is definitely a science making considerable use of numbers, and specifically "measuring" rather than "counting" numbers.

To the student just entering into the study of a behavioral science, as well as to the layman, the emphasis which the behavioral scientist places upon quantification is often a source of wonder and confusion. Granted that it might be appropriate to attach a number to a person's I.Q., what sense does it make to quantify such behaviors as learning, or the speed with which certain words are read, or the degree to which a man chooses others as friends, and they him? Is it not sufficient to state: "Student A does or does not show learning, B is a slow reader, and C wants to be everyone's friend, but nobody wants him?" And, above all, why do behavioral scientists bother so much with statistics? For many, statistics has a vaguely disreputable flavor, a numerical wizardry by means of which the expert can prove almost anything he wishes.

There are, of course, answers to these questions. First of all, the scientist uses measurement or quantification quite simply because it represents a finer, more precise way of describing events than a mere qualitative description. It is more informative to say: "Today the temperature is 95° yesterday it was 70°," than "Today it is quite hot, but yesterday it was comfortably cool." The imprecision of the latter statement becomes immediately obvious if we consider that, had the 70° temperature occurred in February, it would probably have been considered as "quite warm." Some reflection about the progress of knowledge in the various sciences shows that such progress is characterized precisely by an adoption of measurements, as opposed to earlier, purely qualitative description. An initial observation of a very early scientist might have been: "The sun rises and sets," or "If I let go of this stone, it falls." From there, it is a difficult and important road to statements of sunsets and sunrises as related to time of year and geographic position, or to the relationships among acceleration, speed, distance, and time, which describe the fall of a stone.

Similarly, the statements that "C is not well liked," "A does not seem to be able to learn anything," and "B is a slow reader" really tell us far less than it might be possible and useful to know: Out of a certain number of people, how many dislike C? Is there someone they dislike more? Do they dislike him enough to wish him ill, or do they only refuse to bother with him? Or: How many words a minute does B read? Is there any change if we increase the size of the print, or improve lighting conditions? Does he read as fast as the average six-year-old, ten-year-old, or what? Clearly, these questions seek more information than the earlier statements offer.

Granted, then, that to measure, say, a person's reading speed is more satisfactory than to assign to him the label "fast reader," "average reader," or "slow reader," the mere use of such numbers does not as yet constitute statistics. But suppose, now, that we have collected reading speeds for 1,000 words for a large number of individuals, say, 10,000. Clearly, having 10,000 numbers before us without any kind of an orderly arrangement would probably produce a head-ache, but certainly no usable information.

One of the purposes of statistics is to make such infor-mation "digestible." To some extent, most people use such "descriptive" statistics; whenever we speak of an "average" (or, more properly, a "mean" or a "median") we are con-densing cumbersome data. For instance, instead of listing the individual heights of 25 male adults, our purpose might be served by stating that they have a mean height of 69.2 inches. This mean, as I rather hope you know, is obtained by summing the individual heights, and then dividing this sum by the number of measures—in this case, 25. Or, I might be interested in that other important "average," the median, which is given by the height of the man "in the middle," in this instance, the man who ranks 13th in height. (You can see now, by the way, why I am placing the word "average" in quotation marks; it is ambiguous in meaning since it may refer either to the mean or the median. A much better ge-neric term for such "middle" measures as the mean and the median is "measures of central tendency.") Quite often one may be interested not only in some "average" for a large number of measures, but also some measure of "dispersion," i.e., the degree of variation about this average measure. For instance, the mean or the median for our 25 men fails to tell us whether the shortest and the tallest are, respectively, 50 and 84, or 66 and 72 inches tall, in other words, whether the *range* of heights is 34 or 6 inches. Descriptive statistics, even in its more complex forms, aims chiefly at providing such measures of central tendency and dispersion (although it should be pointed out that there are other, more useful and widely used measures of dispersion). There is usually a branch of the government concerned with "vital statistics" of the population, and the uses of such condensations of large bodies of data in education, business, and almost every other aspect of a large and complex society are many indeed.

More frequently, however, the scientist is not really interested in simply pouring over a sheaf of data in order to arrive at some conclusion about the specific individuals that have participated in the study. Suppose, for instance, that he is interested in the effects of a depressant drug upon running speed in rats. Although the "rat psychologist" cherishes his experimental animals greatly (indeed, in the heat of a marital argument, his wife may sometimes accuse him of lavishing more affection upon them than her), it should be clear that what he is ultimately interested in are not the running performances of the particular animals which happen to be in his possession at the time, but rather the effects of the drug upon running in rats "generally." In other words, he tries to draw *inferences* from specific instances upon the general case. Again numerous examples come to mind: The tire manufacturer testing a new substance on 100 experimental tires is obviously interested in how tires made of this substance will perform *in general*. The TV rating service, which bases its rather questionable oracles about the viewing preferences of the public upon a few thousand viewers, cares only minimally about the apparently infantile, depraved, and sadistic tastes of these selected individuals. They claim to *infer* from these samples how viewers "in general" feel about TV. The school system, testing a new mathematics program, is again only peripherally interested in the particular class upon which the program is being tried out; its real concern lies in *inferring* or *predicting* how the program will work generally, in the future.

Sometimes, of course, the researcher may be interested in a description of a group under study, as well as in making projections from that group upon others. But the difference should now be clear: "Descriptive statistics" is concerned with the useful presentation of data about the particular group under study; "inference statistics" or "statistical inference" aims at the more ambitious and fascinating task of inferring from specific cases, or *samples*, to general cases, or *populations*. This last term, then, refers not just to people, but rather to any complete set of measures. Thus, we may speak of the *population* of television viewers in the United States, meaning all the people who at some time or other watch TV, but also of the *population* of "running speeds for rats under a given type of sedation." These two examples also clarify why we need to make inferences at all: in the first case, that of the TV viewers, or in any type of poll, it would be possible, although extremely costly, to interview *all* the viewers. A sample is preferred because it is more practical and economical. But in the case of the effects of the sedative upon running speed, it makes no sense to say that our findings lead to certain inferences about a large, but finite number of white rats in the U.S.A. The term "population" here applies to a hypothetical, and therefore infinite, population of white rats in general. It is assumed that, given that no decisive mutations occur in that species, the findings will apply to generations of rats as yet unborn, and would have applied to such animals long deceased. In this instance, measuring the *population* becomes not merely inconvenient and costly, but quite obviously impossible. Yet, it is not hard to see that quite often we base our decisions upon precisely this type of inference. When I decide henceforth to refrain from smoking, I do so because of certain estimates I have read about the percentage of smokers contracting cancer, and the probability that I might become so afflicted. These estimates are based upon specific individuals who have been studied, and the findings generalized upon not only the large, though finite and relatively easily determined number of smokers now living in the United States, but upon smokers smoking certain quantities of cigarettes "in general."

It is this inferential use of statistics which leads to an often-heard and quite telling objection. It might go something like the following:

"The only reason some of you use elaborate statistical methods is because your experimental conditions are weak, perhaps even meaningless. If you take 20 people and ask them to read type $1/100''$ high, and compare them to 20 people reading type of a height of $1/10''$, you need no statistics to conclude that the second group reads faster. You, however, assert that, by providing certain information, you are producing changes in, say, peoples' attitudes and behaviors. But when one looks at the results, they look very little different, compared to a "control group" which received no information. Then you do a test which shows that there is a small effect of the type that you had predicted, and argue that this effect would occur 'by chance,' or in the long run, less than one time in 20. You then conclude that your hypothesis has been confirmed. But does the man whose leg has been cut off grow a new one merely less than one time in 20, and is it on that shaky basis that you decide that amputated legs in people do not grow back?"

This argument is clearly valid in some respects. There can be no doubt that much scholarly research assesses variables which are nearly infinitesimal in their effects, and the behavioral sciences have perhaps sinned in this manner more than others. Nevertheless, empirical knowledge, as I pointed out in the section on deduction and induction in Chapter 2, can never examine "all possible" cases, and can therefore never be *quite* certain of anything. Although most of our present plans, including the writing of these pages, are based upon the expectation that "tomorrow will be another day," that quite plausible expectation is, while highly probable, by no means certain. And to return for a moment to the cut-off leg, the likelihood of its regrowth is, in terms of existing evidence, exceedingly small, but can we be quite sure that such an event has *never* occurred, or that it may not occur at some time in the future? In spite of possible first impressions, the differences in the decision: "A human leg does not regrow," and "A more anxious person is conditioned to make a simple response (slightly) faster" is, therefore, one of the *degree* of probability involved, or the confidence with which the assertion is made, rather than one of kind. The following example will illustrate this argument, and shows also that the position of unflinching disbelief is not necessarily optimal.

Suppose that I have discovered what I believe to be a remedy for the common cold. (The instance is clearly fictitious; otherwise, instead of writing this book, I should be dedicating myself to the role of sunbather on the French Riviera on a full-time basis.) I have extensively tested my drug upon white rats (for didactic purposes, I am indulging in the further poetic license of endowing these accommodating rodents with quasi-human sinus passages), and I now present myself before a prominent drug manufacturer. The gentleman is understandably sceptical; claims that a drug against this noisome affliction has been discovered are not new to him, and enjoy about the same degree of credence as would be accorded a purveyor of water purported to have been drawn from the Fountain of Youth.

Nevertheless, I am to be allowed an opportunity to prove my claim. Twenty individuals are summoned from their tedious routines of attempting to exhale into a Breath-o-graph (or whatever the contraption is called whereby TV hucksters show you that someone's nasal passages are clogged up); others hurriedly replace the bone and skin they had previously removed in order to allow an artist to draw an animated sketch of their sinuses.

I, meanwhile, am ready: 20 glasses of water and 20 pink pills are lined up. No, I have not forgotten about the importance of a control group, and am fully aware of possible "placebo" effects.* Therefore, 10 of my pills contain no medication, just a plausible-tasting mixture of inert ingredients. I am also careful to guard against the danger of seeing what I expect or want to see. If I (or the manufacturer) knew which individuals have taken the drug and which the placebo, our perception of improvements in the patients' condition might be affected. Or, if it is not we who judge such improvement, it is even entirely possible that we produce at least a temporary, objectively observable remission in some patients by subtle encouragements or hints.† Therefore, someone unconnected with the experiment has assigned the drug to 10 out of the 20 people,

---

*I expect that the sophisticated reader knows the meaning of "placebo effect": It is a change in a person due not to a drug (or, more generally, a manipulation) but to his expectations as to what the drug should do. Popularly, susceptibility to placebo effects has been called "suggestibility," but recent studies show that the type of suggestibility which makes a person accept the opinions of another bears little relation to "placebo proneness."

†This, contrary to "placebo proneness", would depend on a person's suggestibility: such effects could also occur without the ingestion of even a placebo.

using, say, a table of random numbers; the other 10 patients receive the placebo. He has then placed the record of who received the drug into an envelope which will be opened only after whatever improvements the patients experience have been recorded by "independent" observers, i.e., by observers who do not know who received the drug. The experiment, in a word, is conducted rigorously, in accordance with the cautions outlined in the preceding chapter. Now let us look at the result:

| | **Patient** | | |
	Improved	*Not improved*	*Totals*
Drug	7	3	10
Placebo	1	9	10
Totals	8	12	20

In all, out of 20 "experimental *subjects*" (a generic and non-derogatory equivalent of the popular "guinea pig") 8 show improvement, while the remaining 12 will, for better or for worse, continue to suffer before television cameras, on behalf of some well-advertised decongestant. The question now to be decided is: Is the drug "really" effective? It is easy to answer immediately either "yes" or "no" to this question. "Yes," because among the people who took the drug, 7 out of 10 improved, while among those given the placebo, only 1 out of 10 showed improvement according to the observer's evaluation. But it is also possible to argue that the drug is not effective, because, after all, 3 of the people to whom the drug was given failed to improve, while 1 of the "placebo" subjects did! It is therefore possible to be wrong either saying "yes" or saying "no." I may, on the one hand, just have been lucky that the experimental group showed more people improved than the placebo group, and my drug "really" may be quite worthless; lucky coincidences do occur. Conversely, the manufacturer, a dyed-in-the-wool sceptic reluctant to plunge capital into a new venture, may assert just that, namely that the results of my experiment were a lucky fluke, but he may be quite *wrong*; if we continued to run the experiment on many more people, the percentage of improvements for the "drug groups" would continue to exceed that of the "placebo group." This would allow for the progressively more confident inference that the drug, though not invariably effective (aspirins do not relieve headaches for everybody, either), does bring substantial improvement to a large percentage of patients. We can easily draw a schema of the decisions that can be made, and the "true state of affairs," as it would be gradually revealed (or rather "approximated," since we can never run "all possible" experiments) by continued studies.

| | | **Decision made by manufacturer** | |
		Drug helps; Manufacture it	*Drug is worthless; Do not manufacture it*
	Drug helps	Right decision	Wrong decision "Type II error" or "beta"
True state of affairs	Drug is worthless	Wrong decision "Type I error" or "alpha"	Right decision

The manufacturer, as do most of us, wants to be *right*. If he decides that the drug helps, manufacturers it, and in the long run finds it effective, he has made the correct decision; the case is represented by the upper left cell. If he refuses to be convinced by the results of the experiment, and would have been borne out in his decision in the long run, because the present results were just due to a "lucky throw of the dice," he would again have made a correct decision, represented by the lower right cell. But: He may decide to *accept* the experimental results, and yet be wrong (it *was* after all, a lucky break). This error is represented by the lower left cell; statisticians call it "Type I error" or "alpha," Or he may throw me out on my ear, refusing to accept the experimental results, and be *wrong* because, wonder of wonders, I have indeed discovered a cure for the common cold. The right upper cell shows what this "Type II error" or "beta" looks like. Therefore, neither complete acceptance nor unqualified rejection makes sense. Each of the two possible decisions carries with it a certain *risk* of being wrong. A substantial portion of statistical inference deals with the secret of balancing the two types of risk optimally.

The sources of "error" or uncertainty may be others than just the fluke of chance, as we have seen in the previous chapter. And it is quite obvious that the researcher does not cherish error because it gives him an opportunity to show his statistical skills. On the contrary, the systematic or constant errors examined in Chapter 4 would make any kind of an inference quite difficult, and every effort is made to eliminate them. But we have also seen that the very fact that in some instances we cannot possibly take "all possible" measures, while in many others it is simply too costly in terms of time and money to do so, makes one kind of error, the "random" or "chance" error, quite unavoidable. Unless we wish to deal with only the most obvious and therefore often trivial phenomena, we must be ready to evaluate results with some measure of sophistication. It is often the small phenomena, those which are easily obscured by grosser ones, which lead to startling discoveries.

CHAPTER 6

Aims and Methods in Psychological Measurement

CHOOSING LEVELS OF RISK

As I have pointed out in the previous chapter, a knowledge of probability calculus and statistical methods is almost indispensable for the behavioral scientist of today. He must know when to use qualitative or quantitative tests. He must know what assumptions underly the use of each specific test, and how closely these assumptions must be satisfied. He must be especially wary of drawing illegitimate conclusions from otherwise legitimate tests.*

However, such statistical knowledge is not in itself sufficient where the decision which is to follow these findings goes beyond a simple acceptance or rejection of the null hypothesis.

The outcome of a study may have two major consequences:

1. It may serve to enrich our knowledge, or

---

*One example, for instance, consists of comparing differences among several measures, given that a certain difference between two group means would occur by chance only once in twenty times and that the experimenter would therefore be justified in rejecting the null-hypothesis at the .05 level. However, if he looks for this difference among several means rather than just two, the likelihood of his finding a "significant" difference would be greater, just as a chance of throwing a 6 with 3 dice is greater than throwing it with 1 die only.

2. It may serve as a basis for action.

It would be pointless to attempt a rigid and permanent separation between the two, since scientific knowledge eventually almost always leads to some subsequent action. However, for our purposes it is of value to distinguish the outcome of an experiment which simply decides between conflicting scientific theories, and the outcome of a study which is taken as a guideline for specific and immediate action. The criticisms one commonly hears concerning the meaning and use of statistics in decision-making concern almost always those decisions upon which subsequent actions are based.*

Let us assume, for instance, that a manufacturer has discovered by means of properly conducted experiments that a new lighting system would reliably increase production over the lighting system he now has. Clearly such a finding by

---

*In the past few years, a trend has developed which rejects the testing of hypotheses with given probability levels of rejection, in the search for scientific knowledge (see for example Rozeboom, 1956). It is argued quite accurately that the scientist who has reason to favor one hypothesis over another, is seldom decisively influenced by a finding which fails to support that hypothesis at, say, the .05 level. Instead, the suggested approach is toward *estimation* of population parameters. For instance, if problem-solving speeds are obtained for two groups of subjects, one which has undergone previous frustration and one which has not, hypothesis testing would consist in establishing whether the difference between the means for the two groups is "significant" at the, say, .05 or .01 level. Parameter estimation, on the other hand, would consist in estimating the population means for frustrated and non-frustrated subjects, on the basis of the two samples, and within upper and lower "confidence" limits. This latter decision is one which is open to emendation based subsequent findings, while the testing of a hypothesis purports to determine once and for all, with a given level of error risk, whether a difference "truly" exists. Curiously, therefore, the layman has in some sense been shown to be justified in his misgivings of categorical decisions based upon statistical data. However, he is right for the wrong reason, because his criticisms concern those situations in which decisions for action must be reached, and it is impossible to wait indefinitely for further data to accumulate.

itself would not lead automatically to an introduction of the new system. The manufacturer will want to know at least two additional items of information: 1. By how much is the new system superior to the old, that is, by *how much* will his production increase? 2. What is the cost of installing the new lighting system? Quite frequently these two questions will go together. A smaller improvement combined with small cost is more likely to induce him to make the change than a small improvement coupled with considerable cost. On the other hand, if the improvement is substantial he will in all likelihood be willing to bear a larger installation cost. These two basic points of degree of difference and cost, or more generally, gains and costs, apply to almost every aspect of decision-making, including those in which the existence of a difference has been discovered by means of a statistical test. Few people would take issue with this policy.

But when quite similar decisions are made in areas such as psychology or medicine, there is often a wave of public protest. Why, it is asked, should a certain test be used to "stream" a certain student into a particular scholastic curriculum? Why should the results of certain findings be used to accept or select individuals for jobs or army service? Why are certain drugs marketed even though they entail a certain small risk, and why are others withheld even though they hold some promise of relieving an as yet incurable disease? Yet, although it cannot be denied that often these decisions are made by unqualified or biased individuals, such decisions, at least in theory, are quite legitimate, and often quite indispensable. Given that "streaming" in schools is deemed desirable (and this may in itself be the subject of research), *some* decision must be made as to who is assigned to one curriculum and who to another. We must not forget that statistics is simply a tool which affords the observer a possibility to examine otherwise undetectable effects. It does not relieve the decision-maker from deciding whether a given choice is worth its cost or risk in view of the particular outcome it entails. The decision of keeping one's old car for another year is a "risky" decision in that we attempt to pit our projected repair costs (and perhaps increased risk of an accident) against the expenditure of purchasing a new car. Clearly, the greater the perceived likelihood of major repair expenses, or the greater the perceived danger of continuing to drive an unsafe car, the more likely we will be to "decide" in favor of the new car (provided we do have this choice available, i.e., provided that we can in some way or other secure the financial wherewithal with which to make the purchase).

In other words, we know that any decision based on information which falls short of absolute certainty runs the risk of being wrong. We could decide, wrongly, that a new "product" is not an improvement over an existing one, or we could make the opposite decision, that it is a decided improvement, and again be wrong. What can we do to increase our chances of being correct? Let us examine first how we can be more certain of not being "taken in" by an apparent difference which would not hold up in the long run.

One simple way of doing so is to lower the required level of significance; saying, in effect, that, "so far, one has required the difference between experimental and control conditions to be large enough so that it would occur "by chance" only once in, say, 20 times. By doing so, one has safeguarded oneself fairly well against being overly credulous regarding the experimental treatment, but one also has been running a fair risk of dismissing a real, though small difference. Now, if one is more concerned with not overlooking this possible "real difference," one decides to accept, as denoting "real differences," those differences between the two groups which would occur by chance once in, say, 10 times. By so changing the level of significance, one has not really added any precision: the reduction of the likelihood of Type II error has been achieved only at the cost of increasing the likelihood of Type I error. Obviously, a quite analogous argument can be made for decreasing the likelihood of Type I error by increasing the significance level, i.e., by deciding to accept differences between groups as denoting "real differences" if they would be expected to occur by chance only once in 100, or even 1000 times. Clearly, this would be the policy followed where the expected gains of the new product or treatment under examination are small, and the cost of "retooling" present machinery or procedures quite large.

We might note, in passing, that there is a way of reducing the likelihood of making a Type II error while keeping Type I error constant. Again, no miracle is performed; instead, the sample size is increased. Reflection quickly shows that the larger the sample from which we make our inferences upon a population (remember, "population" simply means all the cases with which we are concerned, of which we are examining a limited number), the more accurate that inference will be. We are more confident that a coin is really biased if we get 600 heads out of 1000 tosses, than if we get 6 heads out of 10 tosses.

This simple truth means that we can, in theory, make our inferences as accurate as we wish, by increasing the size of the sample either to comprise the entire population (where the latter is finite) or increasing the sample indefinitely, or, in effect, going on forever with our tests.

The latter is clearly absurd, and the former is often impractical. After all, in the case of a finite population, say, the tire output of a certain manufacturer, the technique of quality testing and subsequent statistical evaluation is used precisely either because the test itself destroys the product (as might be the case if a tire is consumed in a simulated road test), or because a sample of 100 out of 10,000 voters gives an optimal combination of the accuracy of prediction that is desired, and the cost of running the poll.

Both decisions, then, viz., that of keeping sample size constant, but changing the required significance level, and that of keeping significance level constant while increasing sample size, are based upon the costs and rewards anticipated from correct or incorrect decisions. It is obvious, therefore, that the statistical method does not contain decisions, only information. Decisions based upon such information can usefully be made only upon evaluation of factors which are extraneous to the test itself.

SELECTION AND COUNSELING

The decision-making process which involves the levels of risk most appropriate for a given situation applies also in a somewhat different context. Let us consider the following two examples: A high school student has just completed 12th grade, with a C⁻ average. He now wishes to know what to do next; should he apply to be admitted to nearby Hopewell College, which has a reputation as an acceptable, but by no means outstanding institution, or to Swarthmore College, which is one of the great colleges in the United States; or should he perhaps abandon the idea of college altogether and aim toward, say, a semi-professional skill? He sees a vocational counselor, either in his high school or in a private office, is given a series of tests and interviews and eventually given some suggestions as to what, in the counselor's opinion, might be his best plan of action on the basis of his abilities, achievements, and interests.

Let us assume that the counselor feels that, on the basis of the results of these tests and interviews, it would be in the best interest of his client to apply to Hopewell College for admission. The client heeds the suggestion.

In the other instance, the Anderson-Boswell Company is interested in hiring 20 salesmen. The company enjoys a good reputation in terms of working conditions and salary, and it is therefore not surprising that 100 candidates apply. The firm, for all its enlightened and modern outlook, is not particularly concerned with the possibility that Candidate 73 is a hardship case who has just come out of the hospital and badly needs a job, or that Candidate 41 is really a very nice fellow whom it would be fun to have around. In its hiring policies, the only point of interest for the firm is to find those 20 individuals who hold the best promise of doing the best possible job for which they have been hired. The firm may try to make this decision on the basis of interviews with the candidates, psychological tests, trial periods, references from past employment, et cetera, or a combination of any of these devices.

This divergence of goals, between an individual seeking the most promising application of his talents and an individual or an organization seeking to fill a number of "slots" from a larger pool of candidates, is not an outgrowth of the new behavioral sciences. Employers (or colleges, or armies) have long sought to engage or admit those who hold the most promise of meeting whatever criteria of success had been set, and people have attempted to choose the path which they hope will offer them the most fulfilment, whether in terms of money, prestige, leisure time, and so on.

Often no such choice exists. An individual may be forced into a single course of action such as, for example, working on his father's farm or entering the armed forces under the draft. Conversely, the "slots" that have to be filled by an organization may exceed the number of candidates (as may be the case during a general mobilization, or when a firm needs many unskilled and therefore lowly paid laborers). In these instances, of course, the choice of occupation (or school, or whatever) on the one hand, and that among candidates on the other, no longer exists, and all counseling and selecting becomes meaningless.

It should not be assumed, by the way, that organizations always operate in as cold-blooded and heartless a way as the above example suggests. Decisions may, of course, be so tailored that some type of hardship case *is* given preferential treatment, because the result to the community would be highly beneficial, and the organization is motivated by a sufficient sense of social responsibility (and, perhaps, enlightened self-interest) to perceive the ultimate advantage of such a policy. In other words, sales quotas or academic excellence are likely to be highly valued criteria of success for the selecting organization, but they need not be the only ones.

But the basic divergence of interest remains in the two processes, and even the approach taken by a client and his vocational counselor will usually differ from that used in *selecting* candidates. For one thing, the former relationship tends to be less contaminated by pretense or "faking". After all, the client is usually eager to help the counselor reach as valid a judgment as possible, and the counselor has every reason to reach an accurate and helpful diagnosis. On the other hand, a person applying for a job or admission to a college where the number of applicants is greater than that of positions, will almost always "put his best foot forward," so as to make a good, though possibly misleading, impression. This leads to much "faking" in the execution of test instruments and much clamor has been raised, either because the tests are therefore deemed worthless, or because they are said to encourage dishonesty.

Both of these criticisms have only surface validity. Since

the first requires a longer rebuttal, I shall examine them in inverse order.

First of all, deceit can be, and is, practiced in situations where no psychological tests are given. The interviewee with the most straightforward gaze is often the most devious. In other words, deliberate deceit depends upon the motivations and the opportunities involved. There is much evidence that well-designed test instruments, judiciously used, are less susceptible to dissimulation than other selection devices, unless a selection can be made solely on the basis of a candidate's longstanding and indisputable records of past performance, in which case the employer or admissions officer may decide in favor of the candidate without further interviewing or testing.

The question of the real value of psychological tests in predicting a person's future behavior, even where intent and opportunity for deceit have been eliminated, is a far more difficult one. It applies both to what we have generically referred to as "counseling," i.e., making decisions about the best course of action for an individual, given that there are more than one such course available, and to "selection," or the decision involved in choosing a number of candidates from a larger number of prospects. Clearly, if a test, or any instrument whereby a decision is reached, proves to be of no value in measuring what it is designed to measure, its user has, at best, wasted his time, but more likely has incurred a serious loss.

There are two factors limiting the usefulness of any decision-making device, including tests. They are referred to by statisticians as problems of *reliability* and *validity*.

Imagine, for instance, a yardstick made out of an elastic substance. Each time a measurement is taken on an identical piece of wooden board, we obtain a different reading. If we had a policy of using boards of 48″ or less or one purpose, and those measuring over 48″ for another, it is clear that we would make many mistakes of classification.

In Chapter 4 we have discussed the sources of random error. The lack of *reliability* of our yardstick would be one such source. It is now easy to see why an instrument purporting to measure, say, a person's musical ability, can be sorely afflicted with this shortcoming, and why it might make any decisions based upon such an *unstable* and *unreliable* device quite unsatisfactory.

This does *not* mean that the yardstick is completely worthless. For want of a more stable measuring device, it may be advantageous to retain it, even while realizing its limitations and taking them into account. There are methods of calculating the *degree* of reliance that can be placed in a partially reliable device.

But it is the continuing purpose of those who have to make decisions and those who supply the instruments for doing so, to use highly reliable and stable devices. This applies not only in psychological testing but in any area where such decisions have to be made, although in many areas this goal has been accomplished within useful limits. The tailor, cutting material from a bolt, does not worry about fluctuations in his (inelastic) yardstick, and a room thermometer is usually considered stable enough for everyday purposes, although owners of exotic plants or animals may require a more reliable instrument. To sum up, just as a rubber yardstick can tell us no more about how to decide whether a board should be classified as "48 inches or less" or "above 48 inches" than its inherent instability permits, so the value of a test in making a decision is limited by its reliability, but these limitations can be taken into account and the test utilized within those limits.

A somewhat different problem, mainly in that it is less susceptible to examples from other fields of inquiry, is that of *validity*. To return to our example of classifying wooden boards on the basis of their length, we now know that we must have some information about the accuracy of the measuring device we are using, but the decision of classification, once the various measuring errors (of which *unreliability* of the instrument is one source) have been considered, the decision itself seems beyond dispute.

Suppose, however, that we now ask *why* this classification is being made. The answer might be that the long boards are used for building and furniture manufacturing, while the shorter ones are sent to paper and pulp mills. But suppose that in the course of time it is discovered that long boards are really not very sturdy for furniture or building uses; short boards joined together in some way give much better results. Conversely (to carry our far-fetched example a little further) long boards are in many respects preferable for the manufacture of paper or pulp (say, because they are cheaper to process).

The substance of the example is that the decision based upon a measure obtained was faulty, not because of various measurement errors, but because the *relationship* between length of board and the optimal utilization was not what it had been thought to be. The "length test" was not *valid* in predicting sturdiness in building, or low cost in processing by a mill.

If we now return to our example of the psychological test, we can see how this problem may become very plausible. A youngster may be counseled to study music because his father is an opera singer, or because he obtains a given score on a musical aptitude test, based, say, upon his accuracy in recognizing intervals of pitch. Both items of information may be quite reliable or trustworthy: His father is a world-famous tenor, and the test given him has been shown to be stable and reliable.

But how does one judge whether the advice given to the young man was good? What are the *criteria* of "success"? One can immediately think of several, such as technical proficiency, musical originality or creativity, professional recognition (even earnings as a musician) et cetera.

Clearly, then, when we ask how good an instrument is as a predictor, the question makes sense only if we clarify what the test was meant to predict. The problem of such "predictive validity" is therefore an empirical one. We may believe that a given test, or, for that matter, an interview or the recommendation by a world famous physicist, predicts how well a physics major will do in his physics course, but such a belief must be corroborated by evidence, for instance, by comparing the final grades of high scorers and low scorers, or students who had made a good impression in their interview with those who had presented themselves poorly, or proteges of Nobel laureates with their less fortunate peers.

Once we understand this concept of predictive validity, and its indissoluble relationship to the criteria of "success" with which they are used, the frequent criticism against tests as encouraging mediocrity (see, e.g., Hoffman, 1962) become quite meaningless. The test, if valid, predicts, for example, success in college in terms of grades. It may be used alone or in combination with school grades and other information which has been shown to predict college performance with greater accurary than could be obtained by mere guessing. The point is, it improves the accuracy of existing techniques. Now, it may well be that it is indeed the unimaginative student who gets good grades, rather than the highly original one. Whatever the faults or merits of this state of affairs, they are the result of the teaching or evaluating policies used by that university. The test was adopted for purposes of predicting these (possibly questionable) criteria, thus allowing efficient selection, and not to discover originality (although there exist such tests). It is therefore pointless to blame the test for doing the job it was designed to do. The criticism, if called for, should be directed against a system which favors mediocrity over originality.

STATISTICS AND INTUITION

There remains the question whether sophisticated measuring techniques, and the statistical procedures used in evaluating them, are not really a waste of time. It might be the case, for instance, that a personnel selection test is moderately reliable and valid in predicting performance on a given job, but that a skilled personnel director could separate good candidates from bad ones more accurately, with greater speed and less expense, simply by looking them over. Similarly, there are two basic methods available in the diagnosis and prognosis of psychological disorders. A clinical psychologist or psychiatrist may combine his insights in an unspecified way to arrive at a composite picture of his patient, or the results of various tests are combined according to well-defined statistical procedures to yield a composite prediction.

Meehl (1954) provides one of the most extensive discussions of the clinical versus statistical prediction controversy. He notes that the clinician may seem to have special powers useful for prediction. It is frequently believed, by laymen and professionals alike, that the clinician should be able to apply some knowledge which is not included in the statistical prediction, or is not given proper weight in the statistical prediction.*

---

*The dichotomy can be carried one step further. As Sawyer (1967) has pointed out, we can distinguish between the type of data (clinical statements or test scores) and the way in which they are combined (intuitively, and weighted arbitrarily, or by the statistical method of multiple regression). However, the general statements made above hold even when the finer-grained analyses proposed by Sawyer are made.

However, Meehl's analysis of a number of studies indicates that, in terms of the success frequency of predictions, the two methods are equal for about one half of the studies; in the other half the clinician is definitely inferior.

In interpreting these results Meehl notes that there are important differences between what the clinician does during therapy and what he is "scored" for in these studies. In therapy many tentative (and wrong) hypotheses are formed. Even the mistakes, however, may be clinically profitable. For any one prediction, the odds are against the clinician. A multiple regression equation, on the other hand, makes no "false starts." Thus, the "third ear" of the clinician may pay off therapeutically, but it does not pay off in the straightforward prediction of outcomes.

There exists a large body of literature reporting quite similar results in job selection and college admissions. Apparently, hunches usually do not fare well when they override a statistical combination of known facts.

Meehl stresses the importance of distinguishing between formulating a hypothesis and testing it. A clinician makes use of some general laws of behavior which make it possible to order the data in terms of presumed relationships and importance. There may be a formal difference in the process of prediction when done statistically, and when done by a clinician via hypothesis formation. In the genuine creative act involved in the formulation of hypothesis, the statistician has no concern. Intuition is important in hypothesis formation, not in hypothesis verification. In the latter, the statistician should have the final word.

Meehl cautions that any empirical study of the statistical versus the clinical prediction techniques should involve predicting from identical sets of information. A comparison of the frequency of success for the two methods may then be made. In the studies he analyzes, however, many of the predictions for the two approaches are not based on the same data. Also, we must always keep in mind that even the most accurate method of predicting complex human events, such as therapeutic outcomes or performance in college, is still a faulty instrument when compared to the accuracy with which we can predict a solar eclipse. Nevertheless, the findings at the very least dispel the myth of the superiority of "the practiced eye" over actuarial prediction. The proper instruments, in the hands of qualified individuals, provide as good a way of obtaining certain information as we now have at our disposal. The question of *whether* certain information should be sought at all, for a given purpose, is examined in some detail in the next chapter; but whatever the answer, it is irrelevant to the problem of the effectiveness of prediction.

CHAPTER 7

Special Problems in the Study of Human Behavior

Until now I have striven hard to present arguments and evidence for the assertion that behavior, and especially human behavior, forms part of our observable world, and can therefore be studied by empirical methods of observation and experimentation. It should now be no longer a source of discomfort to the reader to learn that the study of human behavior is not in every respect analogous and comparable to the study of objects which is undertaken by physicists, or chemists, or even to the study of animals. There are a number of quite crucial differences of which the sophisticated behavioral scientist is quite aware, but which nevertheless eager critics of the behavioral sciences continue to rediscover.

The first problem is one which to some extent is present in other scientific endeavors, but it assumes outstanding importance in the study of human behavior. The problem, simply stated, is that of the legitimacy of inference and generalization. To what extent can the principles derived in the laboratory be applied to "real-life" situations? Although the scientist is interested in what happens under the particular laboratory conditions he has designed to obtain the experimental effect, he probably wants to be able to make some general inferences regarding the behavior under scrutiny.

Now, as I have pointed out earlier, the scientist, behavioral or otherwise, is rarely interested in the phenomenon he observes in the specific individuals or subjects who happen to be taking part in his study. He is interested in most instances in extrapolating and generalizing from his findings. This is quite simple and obvious, and requires very little justification. But it is quite easy to raise an immediate objection and to say: "Well, surely this generalization can reach absurd lengths. We have already heard of psychologists who discuss problems of the human mind in terms of how a rat or a fish behaves in a very simple experimental situation. There have even been studies of neuroses and psychotic behavior allegedly observed in dogs, cats, and even rats." The scientist himself will inveigh strongly against the unwarranted inferences and generalizations which are so common in the popular literature. Indeed, I spoke earlier with some disapproval of certain popular and semi-popular writings in which relatively humble animals were endowed with sophisticated human emotions.

The issue—and this can be said of most issues that are real, rather than spurious—cannot be settled by *a priori* assertions. Inference and generalization from observations are indispensable steps in forming an understanding of the world, but the question of where such steps are legitimate is often in itself a question of observation and inference. For instance, there are no *a priori* reasons for comparing the manner in which a rat learns its way through a maze and that in which a child learns how to build an object with his erector set. The similarities which might permit such a comparison would be based upon certain *observed similarities* in which the two kinds of subjects progress toward completion, and *inferences* based upon the observations. A unified theory of learning applicable to these two processes would then focus the scientist's future experiments and observations on variations of the two situations; clearly, if he has a theory (based upon certain observations) that the two processes are comparable, he will design different experiments, make different observations, and draw different inferences, than if he subscribes to a different theory.

A good example of the merits and limits of generalization is given by the studies of Asch (1952), which have become classic in the literature of social psychology. Asch used a group situation consisting of a single "naive" subject and several confederates, who had been briefed beforehand in the following manner: They were asked to select out of three painted lines of different lengths, the line which corresponded in length to a sample line, and to do so incorrectly on a predetermined portion of the trials. About 30% of the "naive" subjects were swayed in their judgments, in some instances several times. (Needless to say, it had been established beforehand that these subjects were quite capable of giving the correct answer when not in the presence of the group.) In a later article (1961), Asch analysed his results in a very sophisticated manner, and pointed out that the "conformity" of his subjects can be explained in various ways: They may truly have been influenced to the point where their perception changed in accordance with the ostensible perception of the confederates; they may have come to doubt the accuracy of their perception and therefore, in their uncertainty, may have accepted the judgment of others; or, finally, they may have been fully aware that the others' judgment was inaccurate, but were unwilling to "make waves" or, in other words, to stand out by giving a "deviant" judgment, even though they knew that judgment to be correct.

In later studies, however, Luchins and Luchins (1967) examined the extent to which individual subjects went along with the statements of such stooges posing as subjects who had been pre-briefed to judge the lengths of lines wrongly.

They found that their manipulation was far less effective in producing conformity to the erroneous decision of the rest of the group when they took their experiment out of the "formal" laboratory setting and conducted it in an air terminal. Crutchfield (1955) found reliable and by no means obvious relationships between conformity behavior in a group situation quite similar to that of Asch, and narrowness of interest range and maladaptation under stress. Hovland (1959) faces the problem of generalizing from the laboratory to "natural" settings in an article discussing the differences in results obtained from survey and experimental studies of attitude change. In the survey method, the experimenter typically polls the opinions of a representative number of people before and after they have been exposed to some attempt at persuasion; for instance, the experimenter may check for a change in attitude toward a political candidate after the respondents have seen him on television. On the other hand, in an experiment in attitude change, the experimenter may, say, measure the attitudes of a class of students before and after he shows them a film advocating a particular point of view. In general the finding has been that a much greater measured change is obtained using experimental procedures than is found using survey studies. Why should results obtained using these two methods, which seem on the surface to be fairly similar, turn out differently? Hovland gives a number of reasons for the discrepancy.

First, the experiment exposes to the communication a group of people with a varying range of opinions; whereas in survey studies people exposing themselves are those who are probably already more or less in favor of the position advocated. Less opinion change can thus be expected from the second group. "The controlled experiment always greatly over-rates effects, as compared with those that really occur, because of the self-selection of audience." (Lipset et al., 1954, p. 158).

Another effective difference is the time interval between exposure and measurement. In an experiment the effect is usually measured soon after the communication, whereas in the survey study the measurement is usually more remote.

The experimental situation itself may influence the outcome. If, for instance, the experiment takes place in a school classroom, subjects might infer implicit sponsorship of the communication by the teacher and school. Moreover, in a "natural" setting, the subject may be influenced by discussions with friends and family; while in an experiment little communication with other people is allowed. There exists, then, no necessary contradiction between results obtained from the two methods of studying attitude change and "integration of the two methods will require, on the part of the experimenter, an awareness of the narrowness of the laboratory in interpreting the larger and more comprehensive effects of communication" (Hovland, 1959, p. 298).

In sum, the behavioral scientist must concern himself with the representativeness of his results, not only from setting to setting, but from population to population. In the majority of social psychology experiments, college and high school students have served as subjects, mainly because of accessibility. The possibility that the effect is specific to the experimental population has not been thoroughly explored. As Tolman said, "College sophomores may not be people."

But even within his experiment itself the experimenter must be aware of subtle factors which may reduce or nullify the effect of his manipulations. Campbell (1957) discusses several of these variables:

First, changes within the subject during the experiment may have unintended effects influencing the outcome of the experiment. Simply as a function of time, and independently of the the manipulation, the subject may undergo changes. As was pointed out in Chapter 5, if a psychologist finds that 65% of patients improved after one year of therapy, he must compare this recovery rate with that of a comparable group of non-treated patients over the same time period, before he can attribute beneficial effects to the particular therapy used. The subject may show the effects of hunger, fatigue, boredom, or, over longer periods, aging. These changes may produce an "experimental" effect unrelated to the manipulation. The effects of aging, for instance, must particularly be taken into account when studying young children where neuromuscular growth occurs with relative speed. If he is unable to assess the effects of variables such as these, the experimenter may include other groups of subjects in his experiment who are omitted from treatment to serve as controls. His assessment of the effectiveness of his manipulation then depends on an observed difference between experimental and control groups.

Testing itself may have an effect. Being tested twice on the same test or equivalent forms of a test may result in a "practice" effect. On intelligence tests, for instance, a person may be expected to get a second score as much as five I.Q. points higher than the first one.

Another inevitable effect of dealing with people instead of animals or things are the participants' "guesses" of what the situation is all about. Orne (1962) proposes that a subject's behavior in any experimental situation is determined by two sets of variables: first, the experimental variables themselves; and second, the "perceived demand characteristics of the experimental situation." A person taking part in a psychology experiment is far from merely being a human guinea pig. Besides reacting to the treatment itself, the subject's behavior is influenced by the very fact of his awareness of being a subject. He is seldom merely a passive participant.

The experiment, then, in the words of Crowne and Marlowe (1964) is "a highly charged encounter in which the subject's responses are most unlikely to escape unaffected from the social forces operative" (p. 29). For one thing, he is probably aroused by curiosity to find out what the experiment is about. Crowne and Marlowe observe that:

> "Introductory psychology students probably approach partici-
> pation in psychological experiments with preconceptions
> which are almost certainly not completely allayed by the in-
> structions given them. One preconception seems to be that
> psychologists are *really* interested in discovering something
> about the subject as an individual, that is, how normal or dis-
> turbed he is!" (p. 110).

Therefore, the subjects probably enter the experiment with varying amounts of trepidation and maybe not just a little suspicion of hidden motives of the experimenter. The psychologist is popularly conceived of as a person interested in wresting deep personal secrets from people in the absence of consent or even awareness. All this probably puts the subject on his guard and changes his behavior from the way he would "normally" act.

On the other hand, the subject has entered the ex-
periment on a voluntary basis, and underlying any motives such as money, or fulfilment of course requirements, there probably lies a belief that his participation is contributing in some material way to science and human welfare in general. Orne (1962) contends that on the basis of "an identification with the goals of science in general, and the success of the experiment in particular," there is formed a kind of "pact" between the experimenter and the subject which motivates the subject to comply with experimental instructions. The subject feels an obligation to perform as the experimenter expects him to, in other words, to be "a good subject".

This could be an admirable state of affairs, were it not

for the sad additional fact that what the subject perceives does not always correspond to the instructions the experimenter is ostensibly conveying. The subject may, in his eagerness, read incorrect or additional meaning into the words, expressions, or gestures of the experimenter, and the experimenter may quite involuntarily convey cues of what he expects. The most famous example of this subtle communication, and the degree to which even non-human subjects are susceptible to them, is that of "Clever Hans," a German horse which achieved renown for allegedly being able to perform arithmetic operations, communicating results by tapping its hoof a corresponding number of times. It took the efforts of skilled observers to discover, much later, that whoever was Hans's questioner made slight movements, of which he was quite unaware, and which stopped as soon as the horse had tapped the correct number of times. When the questioner was outside the horse's field of vision, Hans's prodigious achievements disappeared. Most of us have also been amazed by the subtle and accurate perceptions by small children of motives and ideas which a sophisticated and superior adult is certain of having concealed from them.

It is, then, not surprising that experimental subjects can often assess the experimenter's "ulterior" motives; and one need only make the additional assumption that the subject wishes to please, make a good impression (or even in some instances antagonize) the experimenter, in order to have the prerequisites for distorted experimental results.

The strength of this self-imposed obligation on the subject can be seen in experiments in which subjects were asked to perform extremely boring and seemingly futile tasks over long periods of time. Orne carried out an experiment in which the subject was presented with a stack of about 2,000 sheets of paper, each containing 224 pairs of random numbers which the subject was asked to add. To increase the seeming futility of the task, the subject was instructed to tear up each sheet when he had finished the calculations. The experimenter in the meantime left the room. Subjects continued to work for several hours with relatively little sign of overt hostility. Orne also reports a similar experiment in which the subjects persisted in the task with little decrement in performance until the *experimenter* gave up after five and a half hours! There is, then, on the part of the subject, an "active attempt to respond appropriately to the totality of the experimental situation," (Orne, 1962) and these "demand characteristics" can have definite effects in any experiment.

One obvious safeguard against the experimenter's unintentionally conveying his expectations and experimental hypotheses, is to use an experimenter who is unaware of them. This so-called "blind" method, as I have mentioned earlier, also safeguards against selectively favorable perception on the part of the experimenter himself, but it does not safeguard against the subject's frequent tendency to read even incorrect significates into the experimental situation.

Orne proposes a number of ways to control for these effects. One of these is the post-experimental inquiry. The experimenter can ask the subject whether he was aware of the experimental manipulation and whether this awareness influenced his behavior. The problem with this approach, Orne is quick to point out, is that the experimenter might have difficulty in obtaining a valid report because both he and the subject have vested interest in appearing naive: the subject wants to please, while the experimenter does not want to be forced to discard data. Another method with which Orne has had some success is the use of simulating controls, in other words, asking some subjects to behave "as if" they had been subject to the experimental treatment. A "blind" experimenter, who does not know which is the experimental group, then compares the performances. The experimenter is then able to decide whether his results were due to demand characteristics and all too compliant subjects, or whether his experimental manipulation was effective independently of the subjects' desire to respond appropriately.

But the complexities of the experimental situation do not end there. The subject not only brings to the experiment his expectations and attitudes about being a subject in a psychology experiment, he also carries with him certain habitual or characteristic ways of responding. One of these has been called the "acquiescence set." Couch and Keniston (1960) referred to the tendency of an individual to agree or say "yes" indiscriminately to personality inventory statements, regardless of the content of the items. Another response "set" has been termed "social desirability." This refers to the tendency of an individual "to give socially desirable responses to items in personality inventories regardless of whether the socially desirable response is true or false" (Edwards, 1957, p. 108). Assessing the situation, Crowne and Marlowe (1964) remark that there is ". . . abundant evidence that objective tests of personality are powerfully affected by test-irrelevant response determinants — so affected, in fact, as to make the assumption of an isomorphic relation between test responses and behavior in 'real-life' untenable" (p. 166).

Realizing that responses to personality test items could not be taken at face value because of the distorting effects of response styles, psychologists devised a number of methods to circumvent the problem. "Lie" scales were developed to be used as part of a battery of personality tests to institute a check on the "honesty" and consistency of the subjects' responses to items, (e.g., McKinley, Hathaway and Meehl, 1948; Meehl and Hathaway, 1946). Other scales were constructed using "subtle" items, the intent of which the subject would have difficulty in determining. The interest of psychologists was also aroused by the question of what kind of person responded in these stylized ways, why they responded as they did, and what other behaviors might be related to the tendency. Crowne and Marlowe (1964) theorized that some subjects select answers on personality tests describing themselves "in favorable, socially desirable terms, in order to achieve the approval of others" (p. ix). A test was constructed to measure this personality variable, thus providing an operational definition of the "approval motive." Scores on the test were used to explore a number of behavioral correlates of this characteristic in people. The authors then attempted to relate this characteristic to Rotter's Social Learning Theory (1954). Crowne and Marlowe through systematic experimentation have provided substantial information regarding personality characteristics which might be difficult to assess otherwise, because of the tendency of these persons to respond to standard personality tests in stylistic ways. Rotter (1960) makes the point that: "What we call 'faking' is only our recognition of the fact that the subject is taking the test with a different purpose or goal than the one the experimenter wants him to have." In the face of the abundant evidence of fakeability of standard personality inventories, the work of Crowne and Marlowe provides a promising model for research in personality assessment.

Other studies have shown that even the sex of the experimenter (perhaps not surprisingly) affects subjects' behavior, and *vice-versa* (Rosenthal, 1966).

The problems in the study of human behavior, then, are not only complex, they are immensely more complex than the critical layman realizes. The scientist, of course, in the very process of discovering these problems, devises methods for overcoming them. These methods are seldom perfect, and moreover, as the scientist becomes wiser, so does the subject; it would therefore be unwise to look toward any definitive solution. Behavioral science, perhaps more than any other, gains its knowledge by small and imperfect steps. The important thing is that our knowledge does increase.

Another dilemma which frequently confronts the behavioral scientist is the issue of "pure" research vs. applied research and intervention. Unfortunately, this controversy is not only imposed upon him from the outside but frequently divides behavioral scientists among themselves. Some argue that they are, quite simply, scientists. The fact that they deal with human behavior rather than, say, chemical elements, is to them irrelevant. They say that they wish to discover the basic laws of human or other behavior. They view themselves as neutral as far as issues of ethics, morality, and individual and social well-being are concerned. In their role as scientists, they cannot be concerned with the manner in which their discoveries will be utilized, and they cannot, moreover, adapt their research to specific requirements or shortcomings pressing upon the society in which they live.

It is easy to misunderstand this position and to accuse these scientists of callousness and indifference to human welfare. This accusation is rarely justified; indeed we will often find the very same scientists who passionately defend the "neutrality" of the social sciences to be deeply committed human beings in their community and their society. They will argue, however, that this commitment exists apart from their academic and scientific roles, and that their scientific usefulness would be impaired if they allowed personal prejudices of a political, religious, or economic nature to interfere with their research. They may also use a second argument, to the effect that the behavioral sciences are at an early stage of development and that it is simply pointless to seek to apply "knowledge" where no such knowledge as yet exists. The task of the behavioral scientist, at least for the present, they will maintain, is to acquire and organize knowledge.

This state of affairs is not necessarily a permanent one, and it may well be that when the knowledge of behavior has progressed to a stage where it can be confidently applied, the scientist may then be justified in applying it. This stage, they maintain, has not yet been reached.

The dilemma, however, clearly exists: How much knowledge is "enough," and warrants active intervention into the affairs of man? When does the behavioral scientist who assists in an educational program, offers advice in community problems arising, say, out of racial friction, or concerns himself with trust among nations, cease to be a meddler, and becomes an expert? Of course, the same basic question looms when the more commonly envisaged functions are considered, such as clinical and vocational counseling.

If the behavioral scientist responds to this dilemma with less than heroic decisiveness, this can be readily understood when the double-pronged and contradictory pressures to which he is exposed are considered. On the one hand, individuals, schools, hospitals, communities, and governments are more and more forcefully demanding help and advice in their ever growing problems involving human behavior; on the other, many individuals and agencies view with increasing alarm the increasing controls and restriction of freedom. Paradoxically, but not surprisingly, both viewpoints are sometimes advocated by identical sources.

In facing this problem, we must first of all make allowances for individual differences in the interest and the temperament among behavioral scientists. The scientist who works on mechanisms of perception, or the onset and termination of eating behavior, is engaged in as legitimate and important a pursuit of knowledge as, say, the physicist studying the properties of a laser. Nor should he, or, for that matter, even the scientist engaged in the study of interpersonal behaviors, be constantly importuned with demands by outsiders for — possibly premature and unverified — findings, however generous the motives for such demands.

At the same time, even the scientist must concede that the problems of the world cannot wait indefinitely, and indeed become more pressing every day. Problems of inter-personal and international relations, and those of living in, and adapting to, changing physical environments, have to be dealt with now, even if we do not have the degree of cer-tainty in our knowledge that we should like to have. On many occasions, therefore, the behavioral scientist will be called upon to make available his knowledge, since despite its incompleteness it is deemed preferable to complete ignorance.

It is the obverse side of the problem, however, with which there has recently been much concern, even in "high government circles." Psychological research and experimen-tation is coming to have wide implications upon such basic aspects of social life as the right to privacy and self-determi-nation (this last term is intended in its common meaning, and not to the philosophical issues explored earlier). Scien-tists, at an increasing rate, are gathering information which can lead to the control of human behavior. Kelman (1965) points to this new dilemma: The psychologist may justify his research on the grounds that his goal is the discovery of the laws of behavior for the sake of knowledge and also, perhaps, for the sake of social good; on the other hand, this knowledge may also pose a very real threat to individual freedom and privacy.

All of these difficulties are recognized by laymen and behavioral scientists. A number of recent works — some of them bestsellers (Gross, 1962; Hoffman, 1962; Packard, 1957; Whyte, 1956) — have taken them as bases for sweeping attacks against many if not all aspects of the scientist's tasks.

Psychologists and other behavioral scientists, however,

have been neither blind to these issues, nor indifferent to them (see, e.g., Kelman, 1965, 1967; Katz, 1967). Professional associations have formed panels charged specifically with the examination of these problems (see the Preliminary Report of the American Psychological Association Panel on Privacy and Behavioral Research, 1967).

Again, after the first passionate statements have obfuscated the issues, solid arguments can be adduced on both sides. Let us examine the controversies in some detail.

The possible invasion of privacy and the right to self-determination is not limited to importune questions asked by nosy interviewers. Electronic "snooping" devices and computerized filing systems could, potentially, make a public record of a person's "private" conversations, acts, and statements.

This is clearly a sensitive and crucial issue. Even behavioral researchers themselves revolt against some of the indiscretions perpetrated by some researchers (in many instances, it would be quite legitimate to call them "self-styled" researchers). Surely, the logical extreme to which one could carry an unqualified argument in favor of learning all that can be known about a man, must fill a thinking person with horror and despair. But, as Bennett (1967) points out, unqualified insistence upon privacy may on occasion be in direct conflict with society's right to protect itself through appropriate knowledge. Suppose, for instance, that a psychologist, or a lawyer, receives, under the veil of "privileged communication" which has long enjoyed full legal protection, information threatening serious harm to the community? His client may, for instance, be afflicted by strong anti-social impulses which he is about to express in some concrete act or, to take a less frequently cited example: What if a behavioral scientist discovers subtle cues in the behavior of a job applicant which he (the scientist) has good reason to believe render the applicant unsuitable for the position? Is the final decision to be based only on "obvious" information, or does society, or the community, or a firm, or a prospective marriage partner (to cover a fairly wide gamut) have a certain right to know and evaluate an individual with whom they expect to have some risk-entailing interaction? Nothing said here should suggest to the reader that reliable knowledge *is* accessible to the scientist in all of these situations, nor do I dispute that many of the services purporting to provide such information fail to fulfil their promise. It is maintained only that, in *principle*, the issue of the unqualified privacy of one may well result in a serious risk to others.

In addition to the individual's rights of privacy, there exists also the serious problem of possible harm to a participant, even where he has fully and freely agreed to cooperate with the scientist, because of effects which were not anticipated by either party (the instances of such effects arising with the advance knowledge of a satanic scientist are minimal, and will be ignored for the purpose of this discussion). This second issue is a serious one, especially in view of the numerous instances in which deception is practiced to some degree. Kelman (1967) points to several grounds for concern: The more convincing the experiment, the more it is likely that there persist lingering and detrimental effects which may not be removed by simply revealing the deception at the end of the experiment. Kelman cites the example of experiments by Bramel (1962, 1963) in which male undergraduates were led to believe that they had homosexual tendencies. ". . . self-doubts generated by the laboratory experience may take on a life of their own and linger on for some time to come" (Kelman, 1967).

Furthermore, and this is where the issue transcends that of involuntary harm that might be caused, say, by a physician to a patient, widespread use of deception in psychological experiments undermines the relationship of trust between the subject and the experimenter. Orne (1962) points out that deception in psychology experiments has come to be expected by college students to the point where "even if a psychologist is honest with the subject, more often than not, he will be distrusted." Besides the unpleasant effects this has on the public image of the psychologist, the use of deception creates methodological problems in that it diminishes the source of readily available naive subjects.

> "A basic assumption in the use of deception is that the subject's awareness of the conditions we are trying to create and the phenomena that we wish to study would affect his behavior in such a way that we could not draw valid conclusions from it" (Kelman, 1967).

Kelman further speculates that if the subject becomes aware that the experimenter is deliberately trying to deceive him, he might react by trying to outwit the experimenter and beat him at his own game.

> ". . . I would not be surprised if this kind of Schweikian game among subjects became a fairly well-established part of the culture of sophisticated campuses" (Kelman, 1967).

Although many behavioral scientists agree that deception is no longer either ethically acceptable or even, in most instances, practicable, it would be unwise to reject the notion of deception categorically and for every case. Let us make clear first of all that the deception which is temporary and, as far as can be ascertained, harmless both for the self-respect and the well-being of the subject, need not imply a disrespect or a disregard of the subject. Clearly, if we wish, for instance, to study the effects of group influences upon, say, speed in decision making, we cannot tell the subject that this is what we are looking for, because if we did we would immediately contaminate our results. As another example, the common phenomenon of unintentional learning can by definition not be studied if the subject is made aware of the purpose of the experiment.

At the same time it is reasonable to assume, especially in the examples arbitrarily cited here, that, when the subject at the end of the experiment is apprized of the true purpose of the experiment, there is no good reason to expect that he will either feel greatly threatened by the slight deception which has been practiced upon him, or that he will suffer even slight temporary discomfort.

Nevertheless, I cannot emphasize too strongly that this issue is one which deserves careful consideration, not only on the part of the behavioral scientist, but also on the part of the society in which he is encouraged to function. It is not unreasonable to expect that the psychologist is as capable and as motivated to protect those who entrust their well-being to him from harm and discomfort, as is the surgeon, the pharmacist, or the automobile engineer. True, many of his concerns are of such a nature as to elicit strong objections and even revulsion on the part of many. True, also, that both behavioral scientists and those posing as such have sometimes abused the trust of society, and more specifically of those directly in contact with them, by causing unnecessary and immoderate discomfort, either by asking embarrassing and often irrelevant questions, or by inflicting upon their subjects stress and frustration which stood in no proportion to the amount of understanding that could possibly be gained from the study. It is quite possible that the desire to know intimate details of another person's life purely out of curiosity has in the past afflicted some otherwise very conscientious scientists and induced them to transgress unnecessarily upon the rights of others. It is also likely that they have become inured to the reticence and the sensitivity of feelings which most people possess. Perhaps there is even some justice in saying that this new branch of human knowledge, in its exuberant and rapid growth, has produced in some of its practitioners a degree of unbecoming arrogance.

All these possibilities, even if true, would not set be havioral scientists apart from scientists or professionals in other areas. There is no reason to expect unusual asceticism, self-denial, or virtue from behavioral scientists, any more than from anybody else. But these issues do illustrate that no group or individual can or should function as a totally autocratic entity which owes no account to any outsider. Such groups must first of all examine their own motives and methods, but they must also be subject to the control and, if necessary, the censure of society. Clearly, however, the representatives of society entrusted with these tasks must be informed and equitable, for nothing more impairs the progress of human knowledge than control by the arbitrary and the ignorant.

A somewhat more recondite question is that which asks whether it is legitimate at all to control and manipulate human behavior, even where privacy is not being invaded, and where no visible harm or discomfort results to the subject. This question brings us back to earlier chapters in this book, and we shall therefore not spend much time on it. The question is first of all improperly stated. For the issue is not manipulation or control vs. no manipulation and no control. Human beings and their behavior have been manipulated and controlled ever since the first two human beings met and interacted with each other. It is hard to think of any formal human interaction in which the participants do not to a greater or less degree manipulate and control each other. In a complex society, these effects are even more pronounced. Our work, play, eating, and courting habits are manipulated and controlled through education, religion, legislation, and persuasion from the very earliest stage of our lives. The question, then, is stated more properly in terms of whether behavioral scientists should be granted a special monopoly in the manipulation and control of behavior. The answer to this might at first sound arrogant but I hope to justify it. I am of the opinion that *where society deems it in its interest* to effect certain controls upon its members, these controls be entrusted to the expert rather than the layman. If, for instance, a nation or society considers in its interest to reduce the birth rate, then the task of communicating this policy to the people and devising methods to make it acceptable is surely not a task that should be arbitrarily entrusted to anybody. Perhaps the accusation of arrogance which may occur to the reader will be withdrawn if the above sentence is re-read. Because while I consider the behavioral scientist as specially qualified to *implement* certain goals of control and manipulation, I am not asserting that it is he who should *establish* what these goals are to be. This is a far more difficult question and one which civilization has struggled with for a long time, with only moderate success. In the next and final chapter, I shall have more to say about the study and implementation of the "higher" values.

In sum, then, we have examined in this chapter some rather special issues in the study of human behavior. We have asked how generalizable is the knowledge which is obtained in an experimental setting, and how likely it is that findings obtained at one point in time will be applicable at other times. We have dealt with the battle of wits between subject and experimenter at ever-growing levels of sophistication. We have looked at the right to privacy and the right to be protected from unnecessary harm or discomfort. We have paid special attention to the noisome issue of deception, and finally, we have asked the more fundamental questions of whether control of behavior is legitimate at all. We have not found easy answers, but facing the problem is always a step in the right direction. I have advocated that the reader safeguard against rash and sweeping judgements.

Perhaps the best way of dealing with the various aspects of human rights in the study of human behavior is to ask what is the cost and what is the gain. This is not a simple question and I am fully aware that "cost" and "gain" are in themselves terms open to a variety of assessments. But again, a step is taken toward dealing responsibly with a difficult issue when it is realized that, as in most other human affairs, there is a gain to be won and a price to be paid. The instances in which knowledge or other benefits were gained at no cost are indeed rare in the history of human development.

CHAPTER 8

The Behavioral Scientist and the Higher Values

I have reserved the slippery issue of the so-called "higher" or even "ultimate" values until the final chapter. No doubt the topic will once more result in cries of anguish and indignation. For if there is one aspect of human life which has been considered as almost holy and untouchable, it is what people value, cherish, or want. Even many people who have in principle accepted the contribution of science to the explanation of those aspects of behavior dealing with perceptual processes, (simple) learning, and motivation, are likely to become quite forbidding when queries into the determinants and processes of valuation are proposed. Is that position correct, and is it blasphemy to ask whence these values arose and what they are?

Before doing so, however, we should certainly ask ourselves what we mean by the term "value" itself. Altogether too much avoidable confusion results from the use of one term with two or more meanings. As we are about to see, several definitions are possible.

1. *The subjective theory* follows directly from Morris' (1956) first definition of value, which is that of a simple preference or desire. Therefore, to say that a concept or action is morally valuable or good is, in fact, a tautology. All one is really saying is: "I prefer," or "I like this particular concept or action."

Edwards (1956) offers several objections to this theory:

131

a. When I say "mercy killing is wrong," I am saying something quite different from "In my opinion," or "I believe that mercy killing is wrong." One expresses a personal attitude, the other, a belief about a state of the world. In order to make the latter sentence true, we merely have to assess or measure my feelings. The former sentence refers to a norm or code perceived as existing outside myself.

b. According to this theory, the dimension of rightness or wrongness is meaningless whenever I do not make some choice or express a preference. Yet, by asserting "killing is wrong," I surely do not mean that it is wrong only when I think about it, or even during my lifetime. Since I cannot have a preference when I am not aware of a situation, or when I am dead, my judgement expresses something other than a preference or whim. There exists in us, then, a perception of some form of moral imperative.

On the other hand, the objection to subjectivism that many people do, after all, have some values in common, and that this could not be so if they were purely personal and private, is not valid. It could be argued on many grounds, including biological and physiological ones, that other similarities make similarities of preferences quite likely, without making them any less private or personal.

2. Another interpretation offered by Edwards is that of *intuitism*. This is the traditional platonic view, shared by most theologies. It asserts that moral values exist objectively, and can be grasped. They are, however, distinct from physical reality and requirements and therefore cannot be apprehended by the sense organs. What is needed is a specific "moral faculty," or a "moral sixth sense." This theory implies that values are the same for everybody. Absolute judgments of right and wrong are not only possible, but easily made. This is precisely the important point about this theory and the one which leads to its inevitable refutation. It is held that

moral values are not merely absolutes, equal for everybody; they are also simple in the sense that they can be easily apprehended by means of the appropriate sense modality. It could further be argued that the mere fact that people disagree widely about a topic, say "life on Mars," does not imply that there exists no objective reality. However, widespread disagreement about an allegedly *simple* sense perception casts serious doubt upon its objective and well-defined reality. If I look at something, and see an apple, while three other individuals, looking at the same object, see, respectively, a train, a book, and a football field, then clearly any description of the thing out there becomes questionable, and something in the perceptual or semantic apparatus of the four observers, or in the protean object under observation, requires drastic clarification.

3. *The error theory* is defined by Edwards as follows: One can never make a statement about the objective world, only about the state of one's mind: the error in assigning moral qualities to objective events is quite similar to the error of ascribing beauty to an object, instead of placing it within the observer. He then refutes this point at some length. The gist of his argument can be paraphrased in the sense that, when a man says, "This rose is beautiful," he is not merely describing a state of mind, but observing a number of observable attributes in the rose which stand in certain relationships to one another, the totality of which is labelled, partly for the sake of brevity and simplicity, "beauty."

For our part, we have already dealt at great length with the issue of private perceptions versus the world "out there," and as a working assumption have decided that we might as well act "as if" our perceptions correspond to some real events and as if the truck bearing down upon us really existed. Therefore the theory, and the total solipsism it implies, is of no help in our inquiry.

4. *The emotional theory* of values claims that moral rightness means no more than that it makes one feel good inside. Goodness corresponds to a glow of pleasure, evil is equivalent to a shudder of disgust. But this theory leads to a paradox: Something is "good and right" because it makes me feel good, and, conversely, it makes me feel good because it is good and right. Therefore, the rightness and propriety of the concept must again apply to something other than my emotional response.

Edwards finally proposes a theory of *objective naturalism.* The notion itself is not new; it asserts that values are determined by objective or external events, and that these events are part of the physical world and therefore observable. Opponents of the theory have argued that it leads to pure egoism and a complete breakdown of the nobility of man.

Although utilitarianism and the crasser forms of pragmatism fall in the category of objective naturalism, it follows neither logically or empirically that the latter may not take other forms. Frankel (1955) carefully examines the argument (proposed, among others, by the French theologian Maritain) that there must exist in a society certain undoubted truths, unless this society is to collapse. This argument, Frankel implies, confuses specific desirable behaviors, such as altruism, with some externally given set of moral values without which these behaviors are deemed impossible. Allegedly, such unquestioned verities would reduce or eliminate narrow egoism; the "after me the deluge" attitude admittedly has at the very least been a symptom of society in dissolution.

But, argues Frankel, an ethic based upon "naturalistic," learned values does not preclude a search beyond immediate (or even lifetime) personal needs, or a willingness to assess not only outcomes for oneself, but also for others, against one's own immediate desires. Gratification is sometimes post-poned or even foregone for, say, health reasons. I might crave a cigarette at this moment, but I decide not to smoke as much as I used to, or not to smoke at all, because I have good reason to believe that it is bad for my health. It can equally be shown that a person diminishes or renounces his own pleasure in order to further someone else's well-being, for instance his son's, not because of some eternal socially proclaimed verities dwelling in his (the father's) breast but because he has learned to value some outcomes above imme-diate personal pleasures. The theory does not deny values other than egoistic gratification; it merely refrains from as-suming these values to have an *a priori* existence, inde-pendent of experiences, and proposes, in fact, that man can be noble without expecting some tangible rewarding carrot and can refrain from cruelty and selfishness without the fear of a stick wielded by some supernatural headmaster.

The theory does not assert, of course, that values are somehow "out there" as things; it simply proposes that a person's experiences (which are observable) will in some pre-dictable degree affect his most "sacred" values. On the other hand, this line of reasoning does not imply the complete rela-tivism which some discern. For, although the experiences a society or a person can undergo are large in number, they are to some degree limited by the specific ecology in which the person or society lives. The effects of these experiences interact, furthermore, with certain attributes of the person. Some of these attributes are, obviously, universal. Man needs a mate for propagation; children need some care in order to survive; extremes of climate or deprivation are fatal. In sum, Man is a rather narrowly circumscribed organism with many quite basic and universal needs. It is upon this template that experiences impinge to produce attitudes and values within the limits fixed by the organism's need. To give an example of the fallacy which deduces complete relativism from an objective, natural ethic: Some societies kill some of their offspring, in others each child is cherished, and immense trouble is taken to ensure its survival. Are we dealing here with two totally irreconcilable values regarding the sanctity of human life, or can we view these two ethics as outcomes of a) the basic needs of survival for the members of these two societies and, b) the ecological conditions which dictate a strategy of "few, but hardy children, for there is not sufficient hunting," in the one, and "as many children as possible, because many workers (or soldiers) are needed," in the other?

People and societies experience not only immediate, physical imperatives, but also long-range ones aimed at ensuring the survival and well-being of the group. Cooperation, the worth of the individual, honesty, are such imperatives or values which may develop through the interaction of Man's basic make-up, and the physical and social world in which he lives.

CAN MORAL VALUES BE STUDIED SCIENTIFICALLY?

I have argued that the alleged stumbling block to a scientific study of values seems to be their so-called subjectivity, or privateness. Yet, attitudes in general are susceptible to such study, although they are no less private. Sophisticated and valid methods have been devised to study the formation of political and economic attitudes, their social and physical determinants, the manner in which they are interrelated, conditions under which they change, and so forth. I do not claim, of course, that a man's beliefs, likes, fears, and psychological movement toward or away from certain outcomes are now, or will ever become completely "mapped" and predictable, but "higher" values are not qualitatively different from other attitudes. They involve positive or negative feelings, some kind of belief or opinion, and a tendency to act in certain ways. Anthropology and cross-cultural studies in sociology and psychology have dealt extensively with "national character," a summary term for beliefs, attitudes, and, specifically, values, which to some degree vary from culture to culture, largely because of environmental differences. It no longer surprises us that a culture existing in an unfriendly environment, where it is difficult to eke out a bare existence, may develop one set of values toward personal property; if it is an agricultural society depending upon cooperation at harvest time, it may develop rules or norms stressing such mutual obligations. Nomads—and American pioneers—punished horse theft by death; the horse thief was a man more despised than a murderer, clearly because of the horse's importance in such a setting. It is, thus, understandable that we should have substantially different moral codes. Morris (1956) has analyzed people's attitudes toward not one, but 13 types of what it is quite reasonable to call "systems" of higher values, in the sense that endorsement of items in one system is unrelated to endorsement of items in any of the others. Some of these systems are: *Way* 1: "Preserve the best that man has attained"; *Way* 3: "Show sympathetic concern for others"; *Way* 11: "Meditate on the inner life"; *Way* 13: "Obey the cosmic purpose."

Sentences which make up these value systems are such highly relevant statements as "self-control should be the keynote of life" (*Way* 10); or "Affection should be the main thing in life, affection that is free from all traces of the imposition of oneself upon others, or of using others for one's own purposes."

Morris does not claim that his 13 ways exhaust all possibilities, but the point is that there clearly exist more than one set of so-called higher moral values.

Let me repeat once more that the important thing to understand is that such values, as any other attitudes, are not wholly "private" or subjective. A moment's reflection quickly brings the realization that a Catholic saint is unlikely to emerge from the jungles of Borneo, that the noble philosophy of stoicism had a large number of Roman adherents during a relatively short historical period, and far fewer before or since, and that the frequently highly valued virtue of patriotism as it applies to a nation or a linguistic group is a very recent phenomenon, and one utterly inconceivable during the universalistic Middle Ages. On the other hand, the basic make-up of Man and the manner in which it interacts with the environment put certain restrictions upon the values which develop, so that it is absurd to infer complete relativism.

From what has been said it follows that values should be affected by experiences, and we would expect to find social scientists doing controlled studies in which, in a microcosmic way, a person experiences certain events, which then affect his stand on "moral" issues. There are in fact many such studies in the literature of social psychology and sociology, of which I shall note two:

A famous instance of the manner in which experiences or, more precisely, situational requirements affect moral values in Sherif's (1961) Robbers' Cave experiment. Boys in a summer camp were arbitrarily divided into two groups and separated, so that one group never had contact with the other except by design. Very soon, as might be expected, the members of each group developed an intense attachment for their group, devised slogans and flags, and in many ways acted like any tightly knit group. The two groups were then brought together and pitted against each other in such contests as tug-of-war and baseball. They threw their hearts into these competitions to such a degree that severe conflicts and hostilities developed. The groups made up derogatory sayings about each other, and raided and vandalized each other's cabins; in sum, they acted like two neighboring nations at war, each one convinced that God and justice was on its side.

The next step in the study was to reduce the intergroup antagonisms which had developed. The researchers were sophisticated enough to know that exhortation to friendship and harmony would be quite inadequate, but it was hoped that pleasant common experiences, such as eating good meals or watching movies together, would lessen antagonism. Even this often advocated practice was, however, found ineffective. Finally, situations were devised in which the two groups had to work together toward a common goal. This seemingly quite accidental cooperation soon led to a lessening of antagonism, and eventually resulted in harmonious common activities and attitudes.

Sherif and his associates were not directly concerned with the development of moral values, but rather with such attitudes and behaviors which reflect social harmony and trust, as opposed to antagonism and suspicion. But it is eminently reasonable to suppose that, had these boys been queried at different stages of this experiment, their feelings about such "higher values" as, say, "love thy neighbor," or "some people just do not belong in the human community," would have differed considerably.

An ambitious series of studies by Breer and Locke (1965) explores these experimental possibilities in great detail. Exposing people to tasks in which interdependence was varied, they found that such, at first sight trivial, events affected the participants' most important and central beliefs toward religion and Man's obligation to Man.

SHOULD HUMAN VALUES BE STUDIED?

We have come now to the final objection which might still be offered to the scientific study of higher values. Is this an area which would be better left alone? Are we presuming, with Faustian arrogance, to know what must not be known? Or, alternatively, it might be asked: Why bother? Our moral fiber is outstanding. We may not know how it works and what affects it, but there is a good chance that tampering can only impair, not improve it.

The last point of view is easily refuted. If there has been a prevalent trend in current literature and philosophy, it is precisely an emphasis upon the lessening of moral standards, the moral blindness of our time. Good and evil, it is often argued, seem to have lost their meaning, and human life, too, has lost the value it had so laboriously acquired by the middle of the last century. The state of moral integrity and commitment on this continent is, to say the least, not completely immune to criticism, although, for the purpose of this inquiry, it is not necessary to argue that moral values have declined, but merely that they could be a whole lot better. Schein (1958) and his well-known work on "Brainwashing" of American prisoners in Korea, and Milgram (1965) in some after-thoughts on his series of brilliantly conceived studies of morality and obedience, go one step further in questioning, in particular, the role of American education in instilling moral values in American youth. If even a society which professes to value liberalism and individuality produces a value system with little resistance to psychological pressures, then the questioning of educational effectiveness is clearly in order.

In the name of such "ultimate truths" as God, Race or Fatherland, people since the beginning of recorded history have inflicted upon each other unimaginable cruelties. Men deprived of their livelihood or wounded in their self-esteem have sometimes murdered, but rarely with the same unshakeable conviction of supernatural approval and the ruthlessness resulting therefrom. In some instances, these "higher values" were pretexts conjured up by powerful men seeking to enlarge their possessions; in others, even the leaders believed they were carrying the Sword of God. Without wishing to offend anyone's religious sensibilities, it must also be admitted that the Christian ideal of universal love has found only fragmentary implementation, except for a few saintly individuals, and some minor sects. The horrors of the Crusades, the thirty-year agony of Europe in the 17th Century, when vast portions of the continent were ravaged in the name (or names?) of, respectively, a Catholic and a Protestant Jesus, the slaughter of "infidel" Jews and Moslems, all for the major glory of God, are these justifications for leaving these "sacred" values unqueried and unstudied? And are those who claim that "there will always be wars," and "you can't change human nature" really the defenders of human dignity? If I am emphasizing Christian religions, this is partly because non-Christian religions have not played policy-making roles in European or American history. Obviously, other parts of the world are no freer from the scourges of destructive "higher values."

Have we, then, reason for being complacent about our high moral values? The question is asked not for purposes of exhortation to return to the "God-fearing" piety of religious fundamentalism, but to suggest that ignorance about the formation and change of moral values, rather than wickedness, may be at the root of our troubles.

It seems to me that we cannot afford to "leave higher values alone." Far too much is at stake. A complex society rests not solely upon the efficiency and severity of its law enforcement, but also upon the "conscience" of its citizens. This "conscience" develops as the aggregate of norms and rules which the individual learns to accept and to which, even though engaging in occasional transgressions, he pays far more than lip service; without such a code his world and the society would disintegrate (although it is not necessary to insist that these values be unquestioned, or of extra-natural origin).

Can we, in the light of what we now know about how human behavior develops, afford to be ignorant? By refusing to know, we are not really leaving the sacred untouched. What we are doing is placing the responsibility for such knowledge upon the shoulders of other, not necessarily optimally qualified, men. Granted that we cannot hope that what we learn will be always correct, and that we sometimes have to make a decision based upon fragmentary knowledge and understanding, is not such a decision preferable to total ignorance?

I maintain, therefore, that the man who does not fear knowledge need not fear an inquiry into the values that constitute our highest aspirations. Understanding such values in no sense implies their devaluation. In any case, we can never really close our eyes to knowledge; there comes a time when a man must look up fearlessly, cast off the comforting myths of childhood, and assume also that portion of responsibility which consists of unsparing self-knowledge. It may not be always and immediately blissful. But when Voltaire was once asked whether knowledge brought happiness, he answered: "My neighbor, who is a simple-minded dolt, is a thousand times happier than I. Yet there exists no price for which I would willingly trade places with him." Nor, we suspect, could he have, for although knowledge does not afford the simple forms of happiness, it alone makes man aware that he is worthy of his role in the universe.

Now, if I may indulge myself in just one more story before taking my leave: There was once a young man in search of knowledge who visited a famous rabbi and asked him: "Tell me the substance of the Torah (the Jewish Scriptures) in no more time than I am able to stand on one leg." The rabbi answered: "Do not do unto others what you would not have them do to you. Now, go and study the Torah which explains what this means."

In a way, though I claim no rabbinical wisdom, I have tried to do something quite similar to what the rabbi did. I hope your leg is not too tired for you to go and study the many and fascinating aspects of the nature of Man.

References

Amsel, A. On inductive versus deductive approaches and neo-Hullian behaviorism. In B. Wolman and E. Nagel (Eds.). *Scientific Psychology: Principles and Approaches.* New York: Basic Books, Inc., 1965.

Asch, S. *Social Psychology.* New York: Prentice-Hall, Inc., 1952.

Asch, S. Issues in the study of social influences on judgment. In I. A. Berg and B. M. Bass (Eds.). *Conformity and Deviation.* New York: Harper & Row, 1961.

Bennett, C. C. What price privacy. *Amer. Psychologist,* 1967, *22,* 371-6.

Bramel, D. A dissonance theory approach to defensive projection. *J. Abnorm. Soc. Psychol.,* 1962, *64,* 121-9.

Bramel, D. Selection of a target for defensive projection. *J. Abnorm. Soc. Psychol.,* 1963, *66,* 318-24.

Breer, P. E., and Locke, E. A. *Task Experience as a Source of Attitudes.* Homewood, Ill.: Dorsey Press, Inc., 1965.

Broadbent, D. E. *Behavior.* London: Methuen & Co., Ltd., 1961.

Campbell, D. T. Factors relevant to the validity of experiments in social settings. *Psychol. Bull.,* 1957, *54,* 297-312.

Carragher, S. *Wild Heritage.* Boston: Houghton Mifflin Company, 1965.

Chein, I. On freedom and determinism. *Amer. Psychologist.* 1965, *20,* 839-40.

Chomsky, N. *Syntactic Structures.* The Hague: Mouton & Co., 1957.

Cohen, M. R. *Reason and Nature, an Essay on the Meaning of Scientific Methods.* Glencoe, Ill.: The Free Press, 1953.

Couch, A., and Keniston, K. Yea-sayers and nay-sayers: agreeing response set as a personality variable. *J. Abnorm. Soc. Psychol.,* 1960. *60,* 151-74.

Crowne, D., and Marlowe, D. *The approval motive.* New York: John Wiley & Sons, Inc., 1964.

Crutchfield, R. S. Conformity and character. *Amer. Psychologist,* 1955. *10,* 191-198.

145

Edwards, A. L. *The Social Desirability Variable in Personality Assessment and Research*. New York: Holt, Rinehart and Winston, 1957.

Edwards, P. *The Logic of Moral Discourse*. New York: Free Press, 1955.

Ellis, A. *The American Sexual Tragedy*. New York: Twayne Publishers, Inc., 1954.

Esper, E. A. *A History of Psychology*. Philadelphia: W. B. Saunders Co., 1964.

Feigl, H., and Scriven, M. (Eds.). *Foundations of Science and the Concepts of Psychology and Psychoanalysis*. Minneapolis: University of Minnesota Press, 1956.

Frankel, C. *The Case for Modern Man*. New York: Harper & Brothers, 1956.

Gross, M. *The Brain Watchers*. New York: Random House, Inc., 1962.

Handy, R. *Methodology of the Behavioral Sciences*. Springfield, Ill.: Charles C Thomas, 1964.

Hayek, F. A. *The Counter-revolution of Science*. Glencoe, Ill.: The Free Press, 1955.

Hoffman, B. *The Tyranny of Testing*. New York: Crowell Collier and Macmillan, Inc., 1962.

Hovland, C. I. Reconciling conflicting results derived from experimental and survey studies of attitude change. *Amer. Psychologist, 1959, 14*, 8-17.

Immerglueck, I. Determinism-freedom in contemporary psychology, an ancient problem revisited. *Amer. Psychologist, 1964, 19*, 270-81.

James, W. *The Principles of Psychology*. New York: Henry Holt & Co., Inc., 1890.

Katz, M. E. Ethical issues in the use of human subjects in psychopharmacologic research. *Amer. Psychologist, 1967, 22*, 360-3.

Kelman, H. C. Manipulation of human behavior: an ethical dilemma for the social scientist. *J. Soc. Issues, 1965, 21*, 31-46.

Kelman, H. C. Human use of human subjects: the problem of deception in social psychology experiments. *Psychol. Bull., 1967, 67*, 1-11.

Krutch, J. W. *The Measure of Man*. New York: Grosset & Dunlap, Inc., 1956.

Lipset, S. M., Lazarsfeld, P. F., Barton, A. H., and Linz, J. The psychology of voting: an analysis of political behavior. In G. Lindzey (Ed.). *Handbook of Social Psychology. Vol. II.: Special Fields and Applications*. Cambridge, Mass.: Addison-Wesley Publishing Company, Inc., 1124-75, 1954.

Luchins, A. S., and Luchins, E. H. Conformity: task vs. social requirements. *J. Soc. Psychol., 1967, 71*, 95-106.

Mandler, G., and Kessen, W. *The language of Psychology*. New York: John Wiley & Sons, Inc., 1959.

Marx, M. *Theories in Contemporary Psychology*. New York: The Macmillan Co., 1963.

McKinley, J. C., Hathaway, S. R., and Meehl, P. E. The MMPI: VI. The K scale. *J. Consult. Psychol., 1948, 12*, 20-31.

Meehl, P. E. *Clinical Versus Statistical Prediction.* Minneapolis: University of Minnesota Press, 1954.

Meehl, P. E., and Hathaway, S. R. The K factor as a suppressor variable in the MMPI. *J. Applied Psychol.*, 1946, *30*, 525-64.

Milgram, S. Some conditions of obedience to authority. *Hum. Relat.*, 1965, *18*, 57-76.

Morris, C. *Varieties of Human Value.* Chicago: University of Chicago Press, 1956.

Nagel, E. *The Structure of Science: Problems in the Logic of Scientific Explanation.* New York: Harcourt, Brace & World, 1961.

Orne, M. T. On the social psychology of the psychological experiment: with particular reference to demand characteristics and their implications. *Amer. Psychologist.* 1962. *17*, 776-83.

Packard, V. O. *The Hidden Persuaders.* New York: Pocket Books, 1963.

Rosenthal, R. *Experimenter Effects in Behavioral Research.* New York: Appleton-Century-Crofts, 1966.

Rotter, J. B. *Social Learning and Clinical Psychology.* New York: Prentice-Hall, Inc., 1954.

Rotter, J. B. Some implications of a social learning theory for prediction of goal directed behavior from testing procedures. *Psychol. Rev.*, 1960, *67*, 301-16.

Royce, J. R. The search for meaning. *Amer. Scientist,* 1959, *47*, 515-35.

Rozeboom, W. W. Mediation variables in scientific theory. *Psychol. Rev.*, 1956, *63*, 249-64.

Sawyer, J. Measurement and prediction, clinical and statistical. *Psychol. Bull.*, 1965, *66*, 178-200.

Schein, E. H. The Chinese indoctrination program for prisoners of war: a study of attempted "brainwashing." In E. E. Maccoby, T. M. Newcomb, and E. L. Hartley (Eds.). *Readings in Social Psychology.* Ed. 3. New York: Holt, Rinehart & Winston, Inc., 1958.

Scriven, M. A possible distinction between traditional scientific disciplines and the study of human behavior. In Feigl, H., and Scriven, M., (eds.). Minnesota Studies in the Philosophy of Science. Minneapolis, University of Minnesota Press, 1956.

Scriven, M. *Primary Philosophy.* New York: McGraw-Hill Book Company, 1966.

Sherif, M., Harvey, O. J., White, B. J., Hood, W. R., and Sherif, C. W. *Intergroup Conflict and Cooperation: The Robbers' Cave Experiment.* Norman. Okla.: University Book Exchange, 1961.

Toulmin, S. *Philosophy of Science: An Introduction.* London: Hutchinson & Co., Ltd., 1953.

Washburn, M. F. *The Animal Mind.* New York: The Macmillan Co., 1936.

Whyte, W. *The Organization Man.* New York: Simon and Schuster, Inc., 1956.

Index

149